Dr Sandi Mann is a business psycholc
University of Central Lancashire, Engla.... W9-BDL-050
emotion management has attracted media attention the world
over and she has been the Resident Psychologist for the
Radio 5 Live show 'After Hours'. She is Book Reviewer for an
international leadership and organizational development
journal. She has published widely in academic journals, is a
regular contributor to the *Observer* newspaper's 'Work Place'
column and has lectured on the subject of emotion at work in
the United States, Australia, Israel and the UK. *Hiding What
We Feel, Faking What We Don't* is the result of three years'
ground-breaking research into emotion management in
the workplace.

by the same author

Mann Emotional Requirements Inventory™
Psychology Goes to Work

HIDING WHAT WE FEEL, FAKING WHAT WE DON'T

UNDERSTANDING THE ROLE OF YOUR
EMOTIONS AT WORK

SANDI MANN PhD

ELEMENT

Shaftesbury, Dorset • Boston, Massachusetts • Melbourne, Victoria

First published in the UK in 1999 by
Element Books Limited
Shaftesbury, Dorset SP7 8BP

Published in the USA in 1999 by
Element Books, Inc.
160 North Washington Street, Boston MA 02114

Published in Australia in 1999 by
Element Books and distributed
by Penguin Australia Ltd
487 Maroondah Highway, Ringwood,
Victoria 3134

The Mann Emotion Requirements Inventory in Chapter 7 is reproduced by
permission of the author and Ward Dutton Partnership.

Cover illustration Richardson Studio
Cover design by Slatter-Anderson
Design by Behram Kapadia
Illustrations by Ian West
Typeset by WestKey Limited, Falmouth, Cornwall
Printed and bound in Great Britain by
Creative Print and Design (Wales), Ebbw Vale

British Library Cataloguing in Publication
data available

Library of Congress Cataloging in Publication
data available

ISBN 1 86204 464 3

For Jonny Wineberg

Acknowledgements

I would like to thank all those individuals who took part in my research study and allowed me access to their secret emotional lives over a three-year period at work. These are people from several organizations who took the time to complete my MERI™ surveys without expecting anything in return. It is the findings from these surveys that form some of the new research underpinning several parts of this book. I am grateful too, to the organizations and managers that allowed me access to their employees.

Thanks must go to my colleagues at the University of Salford where I first developed my ideas and interest in the field of emotions at work. Special thanks go Dr Richard Varey for all his support and the encouragement that he gave me as I pursued what he must surely have felt was a rather unusual and certainly new field. I am also immensely grateful to Dr Robert Jones of Southwest Missouri State University for his constant support, especially at the early stages of my research, and for always being available thanks to the wonders of e-mail!

I am grateful to Ward Dutton Publishing, especially to Lorenza Clifford, for their interest in the MERI™ surveys that I have developed. Their encouragement has always provided a boost.

Finally, special thanks must go to my publisher, Element Books, and in particular my editor, Sue Lascelles, whose constant support, enthusiasm and responsiveness have been invaluable.

Contents

INTRODUCTION

Hiding what we feel and faking what we don't is so much a part of everyday life, both at and away from work, that you may be wondering why a book on the subject is needed. Indeed, if as much attention had been given to the field of emotion at work over the past few decades as it has to other everyday workplace phenomena such as stress, teamwork or job satisfaction, then this book would certainly have been unnecessary. But workplace emotion has long been the 'Cinderella' of workplace issues, left behind whilst other more trendy subjects such as 'business process reengineering', 'workplace stress' or 'total quality management' have enjoyed the recurrent attentions of the media, authors, consultants and everyday workers throughout the industrialized world. For emotion, seen by many as an irrational process that interferes with and distracts from the rational enterprise that we call work, has for too long been viewed as something to be hidden away from public view in the office, in the same way that the fictitious Cinderella was hidden away from view at the ball.

Hiding What We Feel, Faking What We Don't aims to change all that. This book brings emotion out of the proverbial closet and 'outs' the hidden and secret self that lurks inside us all. Not only that, but just as Cinderella was given the finest clothes with which to make her eventual grand entrance, this book aims to launch emotion into the workplace with a flourish. Emotions, whether faked, hidden or genuinely expressed, should be acknowledged and celebrated for the important role they play throughout organizational life. This book is not only a guide to our secret emotional lives, but also a celebration of emotion in general and, in particular, of our ability to feel, hide and fake.

This view, that hiding and faking are skills that should be condoned and encouraged, is not one that is shared by everyone. Many people see something Machiavellian about hiding our real feelings or faking unfelt emotion. It conjures up images of conniving salespeople tricking gullible customers into buying products they don't want ('but he seemed so nice,' they lament) or even of con artists pretending to be something they are not. But do we all not pretend to be something we are not at times? Don't we all take on roles, adopt personas, or put on an act depending on who we are with? Certainly, we *act* differently with the boss than we do with our spouse, and with a customer than we do with a colleague. Maybe we *are* acting when we fake emotional displays such as smiling, or when we hide emotions such as boredom. Maybe we don't mean it when we beseech strangers to 'have a nice day', ask after a colleague's health, laugh at the boss's weak joke, show sympathy towards our customer's problem, display enthusiasm about a new workplace initiative or look happy when our rival wins promotion. But all these examples of emotion management go some way to making the world a nicer place, to making interactions run more smoothly, to selling more goods, increasing customer loyalty and helping us be seen in a more positive light.

Hiding What We Feel, Faking What We Don't celebrates this emotion management, this unique human ability to control the emotional front we present to our varying audiences, by demonstrating the benefits and advantages that such emotional control can have for employees and organizations. We might not like the idea that we are all social actors, but it is social acting that helps us get the job, keep the job, garner tips, win promotion, diffuse angry customers, deal with distressing situations and generally display the expected emotions that we just cannot, with all the will in the world, really feel all the time. For emotions are not something that we can always feel on demand, and even though our employer may want us to be perpetually cheery and enthusiastic, life tends to mean that sometimes we will be feeling depressed, sad, angry, miserable or bored instead. Yet, if we are to meet the implicit (and often explicit) demands of our employer, customers, clients and colleagues, we are expected to wear the appropriate emotional display like a uniform, irrespective of what we are really wearing beneath. At these times, faking and hiding may be the only options.

Hiding what you feel and faking what you don't is likely to become more and more characteristic of working life as emotional control becomes an increasingly integral feature of the 'scripted' society towards which we are rapidly moving. Scripts, standardized greetings and uniform responses are becoming more and more apparent as organizations that in the past have attempted to produce identical products in different branches or franchises now strive to go one step further and produce an identical emotional experience too. Thus, not only are hamburgers the same shape, weight, size and colour in every branch of a particular fast-food chain but the smiles, saccharine greetings and phony pleasantries are the same too. This is because there has been a burgeoning in recent years of companies offering similar products to an ever-more sophisticated market, with the result that one company's products are barely distinguishable from those of their rival. Employers have learned that another way to enable customers to differentiate their companies' products from those of their competitors is not in the product itself, but in the emotional way in which it is offered. Thus, they each attempt to ensure that wherever a customer goes in the country (or even in the world), they will receive the same warm, friendly and courteous service along with the same bag of fries or slice of pizza. In order to ensure this, the smile becomes part of a standardized set of responses, part of a script.

Whilst this may benefit the customer (or at least the majority that evidence presented in this book shows do not mind the phoniness) and the organization, it does not necessarily benefit the employees, whose continual efforts to hide what they feel and fake what they do not feel have been termed 'emotional labour' because it is thought to be hard mental work. Chronic performance of emotional labour may lead workers to suffer from what I call the 'Have a Nice Day' syndrome. This syndrome is a psychological response to continually feeling fake and phony whilst simultaneously suppressing real emotion. Sufferers experience stress, burnout and may even be at increased risk to minor illnesses such as colds and headaches as well as more serious conditions such as hypertension and coronary heart disease.

It is not just frontline staff or service employees who are at risk of the 'Have a Nice Day' syndrome. This book presents evidence from new research that shows that even those of us who work away from customers may be performing emotional labour in every third communication at work. In the climate of increasing job insecurity in which we now work, the need to be seen as a team player and to be seen as excited and enthusiastic about our work has created new emotional demands previously absent from this kind of employment. It is likely that any job that involves prolonged contact with people requires some performance of emotional labour and anyone who performs this at length is at risk of suffering from the 'Have a Nice Day' syndrome.

Fortunately, there are various strategies that employees (and employers) can undertake to reduce their susceptibility to the 'Have a Nice Day' syndrome and these are described in this book. Using real-life examples of major UK, US and worldwide companies, as well as case studies and examples, the book also guides you through the various ways that companies and employers from service and non-service industries attempt to control the emotional front you are expected to display at work. In doing so, tips and techniques for meeting these demands are given, enabling you to become more adept at hiding what you feel and faking what you don't, without increasing your susceptibility to the 'Have a Nice Day' syndrome. In addition, there is a unique self-report measure of emotional labour that you can use to discover how much you feel, fake and hide at work and you can compare your results to those of the rest of the population I have researched. By the end of the book, you should be able to understand the role of your emotions at work and know how best to harness them to maximize your employability whilst minimizing your associated stress.

CHAPTER 1 EMOTION AT WORK – A NECESSARY EVIL OR A VALUABLE ASSET?

The book opens with a brief introduction to emotion – what it is, what causes it and what role it plays in our lives. Emotions have an important evolutionary function – if they did not serve some important purpose, it is unlikely that we humans would still be experiencing the powerful emotions that we do. If emotions serve such valuable functions outside the workplace, then surely they must have their uses within the work arena too? Indeed they do, and, despite the reluctance many managers have to recognize that emotion plays an important role at work, this chapter presents the case for channelling emotions in workplace spheres such as motivation, leadership and teamwork.

CHAPTER 2 THE 'HAVE A NICE DAY' CULTURE – EMOTIONAL CONTROL AT WORK

The 'Have a Nice Day' culture (or HAND for short) is characterized by fake smiles, phony greetings and gushing commands to 'have a nice day'. Common within the service industry, especially in countries such as America and increasingly in the UK, the falseness of this emotional culture is not appreciated by everyone. New research that I have conducted in the UK, USA, Australia and Israel suggests that at least a third of us dislike the fake HAND culture which implies that companies which strive for the competitive edge must somehow try and ensure that employees not only smile, but that they work harder to make their smiles seem even more genuine. The implications of this extra mental work for the employee are discussed in later chapters.

CHAPTER 3 'HAVE A ROTTEN DAY!' – AND OTHER SCRIPTED CULTURES

This chapter discusses the scripted cultures towards which society is moving with alarming speed. The smiley, friendly and cheerful 'fast-food server' script typical of the 'Have a Nice Day' culture, is only one such script; many workers operate in cultures in which emotional displays are totally discouraged (the 'lawyer' script) or even where angry or hostile emotions are expected (the 'debt collector' script). Whatever the script, the worker must still work hard at hiding what they feel whilst faking what they do not and this chapter ends with a number of tried and tested techniques to help you stick to the script in whatever culture you work.

CHAPTER 4 BECOMING A ONE-MINUTE FRIEND – HOW TO MANAGE YOUR EMOTIONS TO GET THE JOB AND KEEP THE JOB

Hiding what you feel and faking what you don't are clearly vital skills if you are to perform in your job well, but they are also important if you want to get and keep the job. Many employers look for an ability to control emotions when they recruit staff or select people for promotion. This chapter uses examples from real companies to demonstrate the ways in which organizations attempt to judge you on your emotion management ability. Demonstrating your ability to manage your emotions by displaying only those appropriate emotions and hiding inappropriate ones can give you that edge over other candidates. This chapter shows you how.

CHAPTER 5 'EMOTIONAL LABOUR' – THE MENTAL EFFORT INVOLVED IN MANAGING YOUR EMOTIONS

What few employers appreciate is that managing your emotions in the ways they demand can be very hard mental work and this chapter explains why. Despite the efforts involved, the pay-offs can be huge, both for the organization and for you. By performing emotional labour, or hiding what you really feel and faking what you don't, you can make interactions run more smoothly, sell more products, earn larger tips, win promotion, pass interviews, gain customer loyalty and improve a company's image and reputation. However, there is a serious downside to this work too – the 'Have a Nice Day' syndrome, discussed in the next chapter.

Chapter 6 The 'Have A Nice Day' Syndrome

The real problem for workers who are continually having to hide what they feel and fake what they don't feel is that they are susceptible to a whole range of negative consequences to their mental and physical health. Hiding and faking can leave you feeling false, hypocritical and psychologically 'dissonant'. The acting that we do on a daily basis can affect our feelings of self-worth and even shake our very sense of identity as our behaviour, actions and feelings become more and more out of our control. All this can lead to stress and burnout which leaves us feeling exhausted and unenthusiastic about our work as well as leaving us susceptible to minor illnesses like colds. Even more worrying are the studies that show how chronic performance of emotional labour may increase your risk of disease such as hypertension and coronary heart disease. Some people are more at risk from the syndrome than others and the six categories of people most susceptible are discussed at the end of this chapter.

Chapter 7 Our Secret Emotional Lives At Work

Emotional labour is a fairly new concept that has only been given attention in recent years; indeed the entire field of emotions at work is one that has previously been greatly overlooked. Thus, our hidden emotional lives at work have, until now, remained largely secret, as inaccessible as thoughts or attitudes. This is partly because emotions are difficult to measure and identify but also because it has for so long been considered inappropriate even to suggest that work has an emotional aspect too. This chapter presents some of the first attempts to uncover the secret emotional codes in the workplace by teasing out from a large sample of people who took part in a three-year 'emotions' study exactly what emotions they feel, what they hide and what they fake during conversations or interactions at work. Not only that, but the actual degree to which they perform emotional labour can be calculated too with a new self-report tool. At the end of this chapter, this tool is made available for the first time so that you can monitor your own emotional labour and uncover your own secret emotional life at work. You can compare your own emotional codes with those of the rest of the population I have studied and, more importantly, you will be able to assess your own risk of suffering from the 'Have a Nice Day' syndrome.

CHAPTER 8 COPING STRATEGIES FOR THE 'HAVE A NICE DAY' SYNDROME

Now that you have been able to assess your own emotional labour performance, you will be aware of the degree to which you hide what you feel and fake what you don't at work. You will also know the benefits that this emotion management can have – as well as the costs. Because there are so many benefits, the aim of this chapter is not to encourage you to stop performing this emotional labour. On the contrary, the message of this book is that you should keep on hiding and keep on faking. The real trick is to learn strategies to reduce the stress associated with hiding and faking, rather than to stop doing it altogether. Three bands of techniques are presented, ranging from elements to do with the job structure itself to physical and psychological stress-busting techniques.

If there is one aim of *Hiding What We feel, Faking What We Don't*, it is to bring our secret emotional lives at work into public view. Only by acknowledging the power of your emotions and your ability to control them can you really harness them to help yourself work smarter – whatever job you hold. This book is about making your emotions work for you – not just your employer, manager or client. It is about using your ability to hide and fake to help you get on and get ahead at work. It is about channelling your natural acting skill and developing it with techniques from professional acting so that you are better able to hide and fake when necessary, without feeling (or being) false or manipulative. Most important, it is about still knowing who you are and what you feel, irrespective of the hiding and faking you may be required to do.

CHAPTER 1

EMOTION AT WORK: A NECESSARY EVIL OR A VALUABLE ASSET?

THE 'EMOTIONAL OVERCOAT'

'Emotion has no place at work. Be emotional at home, on the bus, whatever. But in my office, I expect cool, unemotional workers.'

Manager

'Emotions just get in the way of the work. I see so often people getting upset so they can't carry on, or even excited so they can't concentrate. Surely they should be able to control all that until they get home?'

CEO

'I spend a lot of my time trying to control my emotions at work. People don't expect me to be emotional, whether that means angry, upset, excited. I have to be the same neutral person at all times.'

Lawyer

'Emotional reactions [at work] are often seen as disruptive, illogical, biased and weak.' Researchers Putnam and Mumby[11]

These views of emotion in the workplace from some workers (and other researchers) reflect the rather negative view that most of us have of emotions at work. The bottom line for many workers and managers is that work and emotion simply do not mix. This is why I call it the 'overcoat' theory of emotion at work: just as when we go to work, we take our coats off and leave them in lockers or cloakrooms, only to pick them up when we leave at the end of the day, so we are expected to leave our emotions and feelings with (or in) our coats and pick them up only when it's time to go home. Imagine how emotional our overcoats must be! The concept of the 'Emotional Overcoat' is reflected in the following ways that emotion at work is discouraged:

- The use of intuition is often frowned upon and seen as an illogical way to proceed at work.

- Saying 'I just had a hunch' is discouraged; decisions at work must be based on rational processes, not emotional hunches.

- Office romances are often forbidden since the emotional involvement is thought to get in the way of the rational work processes.

- Occupations that require emotional work (such as listening, caring, showing sympathy, understanding etc) like nursing or counselling have relatively low status.

- Extreme emotional displays (such as anger or hysterical laughter) are not well tolerated.

- Laughter or humour may be thought to distract from the real work.

- Organizations are more likely to defend their measurable perform-ance than their more emotional and less easily measurable values or beliefs.

- Business schools and organizational training programmes tend to emphasize technical rather than social (emotional) skill.

- Medical students are rarely taught 'bedside manner', which refers to the emotional side of the job.

In all the above examples, emotions are rife, but are marginalized by organizations so that they become acceptable only in certain circum-stances – usually when the employee leaves work and picks them up with their overcoat. There are many documented examples of how specific organizations and occupations squeeze out (or attempt to) emotions from the workplace – and presumably squeeze them into the 'Emotional Overcoat'. For instance, one researcher[2] describes how hospice workers who were hired explicitly to provide emotional support as well as other services found that the demands for the relatively predictable and routinized non-emotional work (such as cleaning, serving meals etc) squeezed out the more spontaneous and open-ended emotional work (such as talking to patients, reassuring them or laughing with them). Another[3] found that many organizations do not even have the words and vocabulary within their culture to describe emotional activities or feeling experiences; for instance, hospital social workers interviewed found it very difficult to explain how they felt because the culture of the hospital only encouraged the use of rational and precise language of the 'statistics show . . .' rather than the 'I feel . . .' variety.

The views reflected by the concept of the 'Emotional Overcoat' are not that surprising, given the fairly negative view that many of us have of emotions in general. It is common to view emotion as something negative that cannot be controlled, that gets the better of us and makes us lose our tempers, start fights or start crying. When we are emotional we cannot concentrate on our work, or we are likely to over-react or blow things out of proportion. Emotional people are seen in a bad light – as being illogical and unreasonable. All in all, it seems that the prevailing view of emotion is that it is an unnecessary evil, a relic from our evolutionary history, a bit like an appendix.

But is emotion *per se* all bad? Would we all be better off without the capacity to feel any emotion at all – at or away from work? Probe a little deeper into the concept of emotion and a different story begins to emerge, as the following anecdotes demonstrate:

'I had a boyfriend who seemed incapable of feeling or showing any emotion. He thought it was great – he thought he was cool and rational. It's true, really, he was, and this is what attracted me to him. He just seemed so mature and calm, never getting flustered when anything went wrong. He was like a rock I could lean on and he was the rational balance to me when my emotions got the better of me. But, after a while, the downside of being emotionless became apparent. You see, he was so calm that he drove me mad! He never got excited about anything! He never did anything for the pure pleasure or buzz. Everything had to have a rational and logical reason. The crunch came when I became pregnant. I felt a whole range of emotions, from fear to joy. He felt nothing. He just calmly started to work out whether we could afford a child, and he wrote a list of the advantages against the disadvantages of having a child. I wanted some reaction, anything, but there was nothing there.'

'I work very hard at keeping my emotions in check at work. I have to – I'm a pilot for a private air carrier company and I have to be calm in the face of anything. Nothing fazes me at work. But when I leave work, I love nothing more than to really feel. At work, I cannot feel anything. Even if the plane I was flying was about to crash, I have trained myself so much that I don't think I would feel anything. My logical brain would just take over. Away from work, the

pure act of feeling makes me feel alive. I love the contrast of feelings that I can experience – happiness on a sunny day, frustration in a traffic hold-up, hope when the Lottery numbers are drawn and disappointment after they are drawn! Best of all, I like to play sport where I can scream and shout and just let all my emotions out. It just makes me feel alive.'

So, emotion may not be the red-eyed monster that we imagine it to be. Perhaps it serves some use after all. But, before we can start thinking about its functions, let us first of all think about what exactly an emotion is.

WHAT IS AN EMOTION?

According to some psychologists, emotion is the 'measure of humankind',[4] or the aspect that distinguishes us humans from other animals. An emotion is thought to consist of four distinct parts and some believe that to truly experience an emotion, all four components must exist. These are:

- What we think – eg our interpretation of events producing the emotion or thoughts such as worry, revenge etc.

- What we feel – eg a feeling we label as being, for example, sad, happy, angry, foolish etc.

- How our bodies react – eg sweating or faster heartbeat, feeling hot, tense etc.

- How we behave – eg running away or punching or hugging someone.

These four components are best illustrated by the examples in the following case studies.

Case study 1

Pat is walking home from the pub one night to her house one hundred yards down the road. She is quite happy, daydreaming about a holiday abroad that she is planning. Suddenly, she becomes aware (*thinking component*) of heavy footsteps behind her. She glances over her shoulder and sees a burly man about twenty yards behind her. She wonders if he could be planning to steal her purse or worse (*thinking component* again) and a slice of fear cuts through her (*feeling component*). She walks faster (*behaviour component*) and she can hear her heart pounding (*body reaction component*). The man suddenly turns a corner, leaving Pat to carry on her walk alone. Relief floods through her and the previous emotion – fear – fades away.

Case study 2

Johnny is working away in his office, when his boss summons him on the phone. Johnny enters his boss's office and sits down. His boss has some very good news and she tells him that he is to be promoted. The new position will involve a far larger salary, company car, plus three overseas trips a year. He is delighted and as he leaves her office, images of a gleaming new car, double-glazing and designer suits whirl through his mind (*thinking component*). He starts to feel really happy and excited (*feeling component*) and adrenaline starts coursing through his veins (*body reaction component*). He is so thrilled that he breaks out into a run, gives a huge whoop and clenches his fist into the air (*behaviour component*). He's done it!

So much for what an emotion is. But how does this emotional response happen?

WHAT PRODUCES EMOTION?

There are many different schools of thoughts about how our bodies and brains produce this phenomenon we call emotion. One of the earliest theories was put forward in the 19th century by psychologists James and Lange.[5] They claimed that the process works like this: we see something such as a lion. The image of the lion is sent to our brain, which immediately directs our legs to run like crazy. The actual emotion of fear is only felt when the legs send lots of signals back to the brain that they are indeed running like billyoh. In other words, it is the *feedback* from various bodily parts that produces the emotion.

This theory has support today from some interesting pieces of evidence. Researchers had people move their facial muscles into positions that were consistent with smiles or frowns – without the people realizing that this was what they were doing. The subjects just thought they were moving their facial muscles randomly. Then they were shown some cartoons and had to rate them according to how funny they found them. The interesting finding was that the subjects whose faces were arranged into smiles found the cartoons funnier.[6] This, argue researchers, is because their faces were sending feedback to the brain that they were smiling and thus the happy emotion was experienced.

This explanation as to how emotion is produced, however, has been found to have a number of problems. For instance, there are patients who have severe nerve damage that prevents messages going from their muscles to their brains. Such people invariably still experience emotions.[7] Thus, modern theorists tend not to believe any more that it is the bodily changes alone that produce the emotion. Rather, it is the way we *interpret* these bodily changes that can produce an emotion.

Thus, for example, suppose 'Martin' suddenly notices that he is sweating and his heart is beating fast. These are bodily changes, but on their own, are not enough to produce an emotion of, say, fear. Martin has to *interpret* the bodily changes and that interpretation will depend on what information he has available.[8] For instance, let us imagine that there are several different scenarios:

1. Martin has just run for the bus. He notices that he is sweating and his heart is beating fast. He makes a mental note to become fitter.

2. Martin has just avoided being run over by a bus. He notices that he is sweating and his heart is beating fast, and realizes just how frightened he is.

3. Martin has reached the bus stop in plenty of time, but the bus flies gaily past the stop even though it isn't full. Martin starts swearing and shaking his fist at the bus. He notices that he is sweating and his heart is beating fast and realizes just how angry he is.

See how three different circumstances can result in three different interpretations of the same symptoms. Only two result in the feeling of emotions (of fear or anger). Thus, this example demonstrates how both the physical changes and the interpretation of those changes is needed to produce an emotion.

Of course, we can sometimes misinterpret the physical changes we are experiencing. This is demonstrated by a classic study performed in the 1970s which showed how people can be induced to fall in love after walking a suspension bridge! Here is the full story:

Misinterpreting love[9]

Psychologists Dutton and Aron visited the Capilano Canyon in Canada which is crossed by a number of bridges. One bridge is a rickety and apparently unstable suspension bridge that tends to sway, tilt and wobble, and creates the distinct impression that the user will fall 230 feet into the canyon below. Another bridge is a solid wood one that is upstream and only ten feet over a shallow part of the canyon below. People walking across the rickety bridge tend to be quite aroused with fear – their pulse rate quickens, they may sweat and their heart pounds. No such arousal is likely to occur on the solid bridge.

The experimenters interviewed men crossing each of the bridges and they tested how attracted they were to a female confederate. What they found was that those men on the suspension bridge were more attracted to the woman than those on the solid bridge! The reason given is that the men on the rickety bridge are in state of arousal, caused by fear, but which they interpret wrongly as love (or attraction). The men on the solid bridge have no such physical feelings to misinterpret.

This study shows why colleagues at work who have been through some emotional experience together (such as beating a tight deadline, winning a contract etc) can end up in a romance – they misinterpret the emotions they are feeling as love!

WHAT FUNCTIONS DO EMOTIONS SERVE?

For something that so many people view of as a negative phenomenon, we human beings know an awful lot about emotion. For instance, when given posed or natural photographs of common emotional expressions, people around the world can reliably name the emotion being expressed. This is because certain basic emotions, such as distress, sadness, happiness, fear, surprise, anger and disgust, appear to be culturally universal.[10] This suggests that these basic emotions are *innate* or part of our make-up as human beings. Yet, emotions must be learned too. Children as they grow become capable of expressing and identifying not only these basic emotions, but also more complex emotions such as love, jealousy and frustration. They learn that several emotions can be experienced at once, that emotions can persist long after their original causes have disappeared and that certain emotional states (such as anger tantrums) are inappropriate for public display.[11]

If emotions are innate, and yet also learned, there must be very good reason why they exist at all. They are important enough to be both part of our genetic heritage and part of our social development. Sure enough, there are thought to be very good reasons why we have emotions. For instance, Charles Darwin, the proponent of natural selection, believed that expressions of emotion serve a valuable, and potentially life-saving, communication function.[12] For instance, if we see an angry face, we understand that the emotion being communicated is anger. We can use that information for the good of both the angry person and ourselves, the object of the anger. In some cases this could mean running away before we are hit. In others it could mean taking verbal action to assure the angry one that we are not to blame for the alleged crime. Either way, without that expression of anger, we would not be forewarned of the danger, nor would the angry one be able to communicate so effectively how he or she felt.

This communication function of emotion is just as pertinent today. How many times do we look to a person's face to gauge how they are feeling? Consider the following common real-life examples:

'I had prepared my first written report in my new job and I was anxious as to how it would be received by my boss. After I had given it to her, I sat and watched her read it through. I was scrutinizing her face for clues and every frown or raised eyebrow made my stomach lurch. Eventually her face broke into a grin and I relaxed.'

'I needed to tell a subordinate that I wasn't happy with some work she was doing. As I told her, I examined her face carefully, trying to decide if she was upset, angry or dismissive. I needed to know how she felt so that I could make my next move appropriate. For instance, if she had appeared upset I would have reassured her in other areas. If she looked angry, I would have braced myself for a verbal assault. If she looked dismissive I would have stressed again the importance of what I was saying.'

The purpose of emotions is not, however, just to communicate information to other people. They also serve a very important self-communication function. Without listening to how we feel, we cannot judge people, projects, plans or events. Emotional responses tell us which things are important to us and which are not. This allows us to prioritize. For example, Stuart had been dealt some poor customer service at his local store. He knew that he ought to write to the manager and complain, but he says:

'I just couldn't work up any enthusiasm for it. I do complain in writing quite regularly when I am treated badly in stores, but this time I couldn't feel any anger. Without the anger, it just didn't seem important in view of the million and one other things I had to do. Eventually, my work load diminished and I had a bit more time. I thought again about my treatment and then . . . whoosh! I felt angry. Really angry. I immediately wrote a strong letter and eventually got an apology and a gift voucher.'

Stuart's anger galvanized him into action, but the lack of emotion initially meant that he could prioritize his energies elsewhere. The emotion served as a means of communicating to him what was important in his life at that time.

Similarly, it is our feelings of fear that can make us realize that we are in danger. Fear is an important emotion since it communicates a warning. Children who have not yet learned to be afraid of 'strange men' will happily walk off with strangers, much to their parents' consternation. Consider the case of little James Bulger, the Liverpool toddler who was murdered by two ten-year-old boys. It is likely that he had no fear in going off with them at first – why should he, since until that landmark incident, who would have warned our children about the dangers of other children? Had he been fearful, it is likely that he would have taken some action, like screaming, that might have saved his life. But, because his parents had no reason to warn him about other children, he would not (initially) have experienced the fear that would have communicated danger to him.

According to some theorists (eg[4]), there are a certain finite number of reactions that are communicated by emotions. One type tells the brain to continue in a current activity when things are going well (happiness). Another tells the brain to stop, backtrack or take stock when things have gone wrong (sadness). A third reaction tells the brain to be aggressive when, for example, a goal is blocked (anger) whilst the final type tells the brain to stop and pay attention to the dangers in the environment caused by a threat (fear).

Emotions can also have functions other than communicating to ourselves or to other people. Sadness, for instance, is an emotion that causes us to 'disengage' or reduce our involvement in the cause of our emotion. Thus, if our partner has left us, the emotion of sadness will eventually help us to disengage from that person and get on with our life. Similarly, in bereavement, sadness is the emotion of disengagement from the lost relationship.[4] The emotion contributes to this disengagement process by helping us recall similar times when we were sad; researchers have shown that when we are sad or depressed, we are more likely to remember other episodes of sadness or depression.[13] Whilst this may in the short term make us feel worse, in the long term, this emotional memory may allow us to backtrack and realize that there were other times when we felt just as bad, but we managed to get on with our lives then and so we will do so again. Of course, the sadness, when communicated to others, also elicits support and sympathy which further helps the person with their loss.

WHAT ROLE CAN EMOTION PLAY AT WORK?

So much for the role of emotions in everyday life, but what about the role they play in the workplace? Far from emotion being irrelevant at work as so many people would like to believe, emotion actually has a very important role to play and its functions go beyond that of the communicative or informative purposes that it may hold outside work. In other words, emotion may have some valuable purpose in life generally, but at work, it takes on extra significance.

Role of emotion in workplace motivation

Motivation is a basic psychological process that drives us in what we do. In the workplace, we can be motivated by many things, ranging from the pay packet at the end of the month (or day or week), to the need for status provided by a high-powered job.

All human beings are motivated by primary or basic motives. Such motives are usually unlearned and include such things as water and food. At the very basic level, we are driven by the need to satisfy our thirst and our hunger. When these needs are satisfied, as they generally are much of the time in Western cultures, different motives will drive us. Thus, we may then be motivated by the need for reward or status, love or friendship. Consider the following case study as an illustration of the hierarchy of motives that can govern how we work:

Case study

Alex arrives at work at 9am and settles down to finish a report he has to write. He hates writing reports, but knows that if he does it, he will be able to move on and do a piece of work he does like. Also, if he does it well, his boss will be pleased with him, and in the long term, this may contribute towards his prospects of promotion and increased salary and status, both of which are important to him. By 1pm, however, his stomach is rumbling, and all he can think about is lunch. His desire for promotion and pleasing his boss no longer seem so important and he leaves his desk to go in search of a sandwich.

Clearly, Alex is motivated at the basic level by food and this need must be satisfied before he will be motivated by anything else. Then, there is a hierarchy of motives that drive him, from the immediate reward of being able to move on to another more interesting piece of work, to the longer-term reward of being able to command a better salary. This concept of a hierarchy of motives was first proposed by Maslow in 1954[14] and applied to work motivation a little later.

Although not everyone is motivated by the same hierarchy of needs – a factory worker may be more than content with routinized work that ensures a steady pay packet, whilst a business entrepreneur may be motivated by making her dreams reality rather than earning a steady wage – many psychologists and managers hold the view that people are motivated by reward of some kind. At work we are motivated by an exchange of our effort for the reward we want – whatever that might be. If the reward is worth it, we will put more effort in. If we think we are likely to get the reward, we will put more effort in than if we are unsure if we will ever be rewarded at all. The table shows examples of the various motivation-reward systems that may operate at work.

Effort	Rewards/Motivators
Working late or at weekends	Prospects of promotion
Doing a favour for a colleague	Expectation of favour being returned
Working overtime	Extra pay
Taking more responsibility	Status

These approaches to motivation suggest that essentially the employee trades effort for reward and this is what motivates them. However, this is not the full story and there are many instances that demonstrate how emotional involvement can be central to motivation. For instance, people at work often perform tasks that appear to go above and beyond the reward and exchange systems described above. They volunteer for unpopular tasks, help others, take work home with them, do work outside their job role and even take lower pay. This is because, in time, an emotional commitment (to others in the organization and to the organization as a whole) takes over the more calculated reward–exchange systems that motivate people. Emotions such as enthusiasm, interest and excitement become more central to the job than more tangible rewards.

The following case study illustrates how this emotional connection can be central to motivation at work:

Case study

Susan worked for a charitable trust, involved in providing provision for disadvantaged youngsters. She was appointed at a suitable salary and her hours and conditions agreed. After a year, during which she grew very attached to the youngsters and her work, the trust came into financial difficulties. The trust manager explained to Susan that the future was not certain and if she wished to look for alternative employment, he would understand. However, the trust was making several applications to funding bodies to enable them to survive.

Susan decided to go part-time in order to stretch the money available out longer. She also declined an inflationary pay-rise due to her. She worked like this for eight months, invariably working full-time most weeks in order to get all the work done. After eight months, the trust was given a large pay award from a charity board and Susan went back to full-time pay and received her pay awards.

What Susan did in terms of traditional approaches to motivation did not make sense. She should have been motivated by money – a basic motivator – but instead, her emotional commitment to the job turned out to be her real motivator. When the chips were down, she would rather forsake the money than her emotional involvement with the youngsters.

There are many ways that emotional involvement at work can become the motivating factor, rather than traditional reward, as the following table illustrates:

Effort	Role of emotion in motivator
Helping colleague	Although the helper may expect a return favour, they may also help because they have grown to like and respect that colleague. People in these circumstances will even help colleagues who are in the process of leaving and thus cannot repay the favour. They are motivated by an emotional attachment to the colleague.
Working late into the night	This may not just be for the reward of praise or potential promotion. The worker could have an emotional responsibility to the company or to colleagues to produce the work on time. In other words, they would *feel* bad if they let their colleagues down.
Perform work that is not in job description	Again, many workers do tasks that are not strictly required of them, such as conducting surveys, arranging lunches, even moving furniture! They are unlikely to be rewarded for such tasks in terms of promotion, but are more likely to do so out of an emotional need to help and be helpful.

Without the presence of emotion, then, it is unlikely that we would be as committed and motivated to the organization. Managers who really want their staff to be motivated, enthused and excited by the work should clearly not be encouraging workers to leave their emotions in their metaphorical 'Emotional Overcoats'.

Role of emotion in leadership

'Leaders communicate their vision to those around them in ways that emotionally enroll others'[15]

'Leadership is about emotion'[16]

The role of emotion in leadership is very much related to its role in motivation. For an effective leader will encourage followers to act in desired ways, not because they are offering some physical reward such as money, but because they have *emotionally engaged* the worker. Consider this case study:

Case study

A supermarket in the north of England was managed within two team divisions so that one manager was responsible for workers on the afternoon shifts and another on the morning shifts. As an experiment, the store was going to open all night every Friday. The two managers were told to ensure that there were sufficient 'volunteers' to staff the store throughout the night. Although the staff would be paid time and a half, no other financial incentives could be offered.

The first manager operated on a reward–exchange system. He was cool and aloof with his staff. He expected the staff to work hard in return for money. He called a meeting and told his staff what would be happening. He stressed what was in it for them; opportunities to earn some extra money that they could put towards Christmas. He asked for volunteers, and those who needed the cash more than a good night's sleep volunteered.

The second manager operated on an emotional level. She was emotionally involved with the staff, often asking them about their families and work-related problems. She called a meeting and stressed how exciting the new developments were, as theirs would be the first store to open all night in the area. She also told them how enthusiastic she was about the project and said that she would be there each Friday night as she was interested to see who came to shop. She asked for volunteers, and, although some volunteered just for the money, a few workers offered to give it a go because it sounded like fun.

The second manager had managed to enthuse her staff with emotion that meant that they were working for some greater good or reason rather than just financial.

Leaders who use emotion are often great believers in mission statements and in the guiding values of the company. These are the 'touchy-feely' aspects of the organization that stress how customers or employees should be treated. They tend to use emotional language, enthusiastic tones of voice and animated speech in order to communicate their values, beliefs and aims. Emotional leaders use metaphors, stories, myths and rituals to communicate and enthuse, rather than statistics, facts and dry information. Consider the following examples of a speech from two leaders, one for whom emotion plays a central role and one for whom emotions are stored every day in his 'Emotional Overcoat'.

1. *'We are meeting today to discuss the future of the ABC Corporation. This is an organization which began with one man sixty years ago and has grown to a thousand-strong team. Picture the scene, all those years ago, of a young boy, barely out of school, taking his barrow to the fish market in the early hours of the morning to pick the freshest produce, then wheeling it back along the dusty roads to his pitch on the High Street. Imagine his joy when he bought his first store, took on his first assistant . . . and sold his company forty years later for two million pounds. Thanks to him, ABC is now the leading fish supplier in the UK and our performance last year indicates that his strategy of supplying the freshest produce at the lowest price still holds true. But our work is not done yet. We mustn't rest on our laurels and lick our lips like a contented cat. No, we have more work to do yet, if we are to take this company to the next millennium.'*

2. *'We are meeting today to discuss the future of the ABC Corporation. Over the last sixty years this company has gone from strength to strength, with a personnel increase of over a thousand per cent. In that time our turnover has also increased well over five thousand per cent and in the last year alone we sold more fish than any of our competitors. But we must develop a new long-term strategy to ensure that we stay Number One.'*

See how more motivating Leader 1 is with his acceptance of the role of emotion in his speech. By using emotional language, he stimulates the emotional responses of excitement, enthusiasm and interest in his followers. These emotions are more likely to be translated into action in pursuit of the organizational goals that the leader outlines than is the emotionless language of Leader 2.

Role of emotion in group dynamics at work

Few people exist in isolation at work. Most of us work with other people, either in close physical proximity (sharing an office or office space), in teams or in groups. We interact with colleagues, bosses, subordinates, people from different branches, different departments etc constantly, whether by phone, face-to-face, meeting, letter, fax or e-mail.

Any interaction with other people involves some sort of group 'dynamic'. This refers to the process involved in the formation, maintenance and performance of groups and these groups can be formal, as in work teams, or informal, as in everyone who works in Department A.

One 'dynamic' that is thought to be crucial to a group's survival and success is 'cohesiveness' or attraction of each group member to others in the group. Thus, a group is likely to perform well if members of the group like each other. This liking is an emotional property and may have little to do with what members can offer each other in terms of rewards. Some organizations rely on this emotional bond between members in order to improve task effectiveness. For instance, armies typically rely on a soldier's loyalty to his or her platoon rather than to the army as an institution. Similarly, many organizations rely on the social pressures exerted by group members to induce newcomers to perform tasks that go beyond the job description. The following anecdote serves as an example:

> 'I manage several work-teams of between five and ten people each. The first thing I do when I start doing team-building with each group is start to develop an emotional bond between members. I think it is really important for members to like each other and want to do things that will benefit each other. If they actually enjoy work-ing with each other, and they care to some degree about each other, they are more likely to do things that will benefit the group, rather than just themselves.' Team Manager

The role of emotion in group dynamics is even more important when we consider a phenomenon called *emotional contagion*. This has been described as is the 'tendency to mimic another person's emotional experience/expression'.[17] According to another source, we catch emo-tions from on another 'as though they were a kind of social virus'.[18] This could explain the effectiveness of advertising in which happy, smiling models are used, why 'canned laughter' is often used in mediocre tele-vision comedies and why 'claques' of professional applauders at the-atres are sometimes used to induce and spread admiration of the show or performers. There are rumours that even some celebrities hire professional 'fans' to induce feelings of admiration from passersby.

Emotional contagion in the workplace underlies such phrases as 'team spirit', 'electricity in the air' and 'esprit de corps' and can be illustrated by the following anecdotal examples:

> 'I have a colleague at work who is always miserable. She always finds something to moan about, whether it's the weather, the work, the boss or her boyfriend. I don't know why it is, but I invariably

end up feeling as miserable as her! I think once she starts moaning about the weather, she brings home to me the fact that it's been so cold for so long – I don't think I would have noticed before. Similarly, when she moans about her boyfriend, it reminds me that my own husband has his failings too.'

'Have you ever noticed that if someone in a meeting yawns, you suddenly feel tired and bored? I have seen this feeling whip around an entire room full of people who can go from interested to lethargic within minutes. At this point, I try and inject some enthusiasm to get them going again.'

'We have an office next door where the secretaries are always having a laugh. It's strange, but the rest of us often find ourselves wandering in there – perhaps we need cheering up, but we do seem to catch their humour.'

'If you do someone a favour, that is, you are nice to them, they will be nice to someone else! Try it! For instance, if someone lets you in the road, that makes you feel happy, so you let the next car in . . . then they feel happy, and on it goes. That's why they say "spread a little happiness!"[7]*'*

But why are emotions so catching? There are a number of possible explanations:

- Someone else's emotional experiences trigger off memories of our own similar experiences. Thus, when the person quoted above heard her colleague complain about her boyfriend, this made her remember the problems she was experiencing with her husband. Similarly, if we hear someone talking about the death of a parent, this can trigger memories of the death of our own parent, and we become sad. It seems like we have 'caught' their emotion, but what has actually happened is that their emotion has triggered our own emotional memories.

- Another explanation could be that we learn to associate certain things with certain emotions. This is a conditioning response which happens when we learn to associate one event with another. For example, we learn very early on as babies to associate mother with food; we are *conditioned* to associate nurturing with mothers (and, by generalization, all women). So, imagine that a child experiences a violent father whose rage stimulates fear in her. This is a conditioned association and can be generalized so that whenever she sees any angry or distressed person, she feels fear or distress. As an adult, this association remains, so that if she sees a distressed person, she becomes distressed herself.

- A final explanation could lie in the very human process of mimicking that we engage in from our early days as infants. As babies we learn to synchronize our movements with our parents, in order to strengthen the bond between us. As we grow, we mimic their facial expressions and are rewarded when we smile at them. This continues into adulthood, so that when others smile, we do too. When others look sad, we adopt a similar expression out of sympathy. Now, remember the early section on how emotions are produced? It is the physical changes in our bodies, such as smiling, that are partly responsible for the emotion we feel. So, if we smile, we are more likely to feel happy! Thus, the emotion is caught!

According to some psychologists[19] we are more likely to 'catch' emotions at work under the following conditions:

- When we interact a lot with the other person: a one-off meeting with a sad person will not be very likely to influence us.

- When we like the other person: we are more likely to catch emotions off people we like and are quite similar to than people we dislike or who are very dissimilar to us.

- When an emotion is clearly expressed by a popular or high-status person: thus, we are more likely to catch our boss's emotion than our subordinate's.

- When the emotion is one that it is appropriate to express at work (see later chapters).

- When we do not already feel strong emotions that contrast with the 'catching' emotion: if we feel incredibly happy on a day when our colleague turns up for work in acute misery, we are less likely to catch their misery.

- When we are not entirely sure about which emotions we should be expressing: so we look to others for guidance.

The role of emotion in the workplace can clearly be seen in this chapter to have great importance. In every interaction or conversation we have at work, the emotions we display can have powerful effects on other people. This is because displayed emotions serve as a form of communication between the sender and receiver. Emotions expressed by workers can thus influence the behaviour of the people who are the targets of the emotional expression. This is why it is generally believed that friendly employees can attract customers and encourage them to spend more money, whilst rude employees can drive customers away. Similarly, police interrogators convey negative and esteem-degrading emotions to suspects in an effort to get them to confess,[20] professional poker players display neutral emotions whatever they really feel[21] and smiling nuns soliciting for charitable donations at stations can earn larger sums than glum ones.[22]

Because emotions at work play such an important role, many managers and companies go to great lengths to control which emotions employees display, when and even for how long. This control can be quite formal (and examples of this will be given later) or just loosely bound up in the culture of the organization. Just as society has certain rules about our emotional displays in public (such as 'don't laugh out loud on the bus or others will think you strange'), so organizations can have expectations that dictate emotional expression (such as 'lawyers in this company should appear cool and emotionless to clients'). So, only a limited range of emotional expression tends to be socially acceptable in the workplace. Expressions of negative emotion such as fear, anxiety and anger tend to be unacceptable, as do expressions of intense emotion – except under certain conditions such as celebrating an increased profit in the year. These expectations about which emotions should or should not be displayed will be discussed in the next chapter.

CHAPTER 2

THE 'HAVE A NICE DAY' CULTURE: EMOTIONAL CONTROL AT WORK

'You are now professional people. When you open your caravan door in the morning, just because you haven't got your uniform on . . . there's going to be people walking past who have seen you on that stage the night before, and to them you are still on stage. And that takes getting used to. You've got to remember it's now a stage. And smile if you're on stage!' Haven Holiday Camps Entertainment's Manager, Ian Sandy, talking to new Havenmate recruits. Broadcast on Channel 4 Television, 1 February 1996.

'Workers are increasingly expected to control their emotions on the job.'[1]

'As a farmer puts blinkers on his workhorse to guide its vision forward, so institutions manage how we feel.'[2]

'I want you to go out there and really smile. Your smile is your biggest asset. I want you to go out there and use it. Smile. Really smile. Really lay it on.' Trainer at Delta Airlines Stewardess Training Center[3]

'Police officers are instructed and trained to curb their anger when under provocation; the clergy are expected to show compassion, whatever; probation officers are expected to work sympathetically with clients, regardless of what they feel about their misdemeanours; and doctors are supposed to react coolly and dispassionately to whatever ailments their patients bring.'[4]

'Some emotions are suppressed because they do not show us in a favourable light, while others, not actually felt, may be manufactured if social circumstances demand. Generally, negative emotions such as misery and hate are suppressed, while positive, friendly ones are faked or exaggerated when we are in public.'[5]

All the above quotes demonstrate the many ways and circumstances in which employers attempt to control the emotions that their employees display on a day-to-day basis at work. Most of these displayed emotions are positive, cheerful and upbeat ones and the result is what I call the 'Have a Nice Day' culture, characterized by fake smiles, forced *bonhomie*, and meaningless demands by workers to 'have a nice day'. The 'Have a Nice Day' culture, or HAND culture for short, is part of the development of a *scripted culture* that I believe Western society seems to be moving towards. This scripted culture (which will be discussed in greater detail in the next chapter) is typified by the following:

- Those scripted greetings that many receptionists now employ when answering the phone: for example, 'Hello-thanks-for-calling-Hotel-Happy-my-name-is-Tracey-how-may-I-help-you?'

- The scripts that fast-food workers are given to ensure that they ask customers if they want, for example, fries or a drink with their order. This can easily be demonstrated the next time you visit a burger joint; ask for a burger 'no fries' and wait for the automatic scripted response, 'Would you like fries with that?'.

- The vague enquiries into our health that we encounter on a day-to-day basis. See what happens if you reply, 'No I'm not very well today'. This deviation from the script will cause most workers to flounder.

- The literal scripts on voicemail systems that are commonplace in so many companies now: 'Press 1 for a sales enquiry, press 2 for an after-care enquiry, press 3 . . .'

Most of us are very well aware, however, that the emotional displays that are part of the HAND culture may well be fake. For instance, ask yourself the following questions:

- When a fast-food server at your local hamburger joint smiles at you, is it because they like you?

- When the cashier at your supermarket tells you to 'have a nice day', does he or she mean it?

- When your subordinate laughs at your not-so-funny joke, is it because they are really amused?

- When your colleague expresses sympathy because your cat has died, is it genuine?

- When the bus driver tells you to 'cheer up – it may never happen', does he or she really care?

- When the store assistant asks 'how are you today?', are they interested in your answer?

The answer to all these questions, as most of us know, is probably 'no'. We know that employers demand that workers create a HAND culture by displaying or expressing interest, sympathy, warmth or friendliness even if they don't feel like it. Workers have to work hard at controlling the emotions they present to the outside world, in order that they meet the demands of their boss or the customer or just in order to meet society's expectations that their emotional display matches the corporate image. Most organizations nowadays, especially those in the service sector, attempt to cultivate a corporate image that strongly suggests the service culture they are trying to project. A strong service culture means that staff are happy and pleased to help, enjoy their work, like the company and will always deal pleasantly with customers. Thus, a company that advertises its happy, smiling staff will not tolerate a sulky, frowning employee because there would then be a discrepancy between the corporate image and reality. Moreover, generalization effects mean that the customer who encounters just one miserable employee is likely to feel that the entire company is miserable (conversely, one happy employee can quickly create the impression that the entire company is happy). This is why employers are highly intolerant of employees displaying the wrong emotions. This can, of course, lead to what one source refers to as the 'forced, unnatural quality of the fake smile'[6] but this will be returned to later. First, consider the following real-life case studies from workers struggling to maintain the HAND culture:

Case study 1

Lorraine is a receptionist for a large hospital and has worked there for five years. Recently, the introduction of the Patient's Charter has meant some changes in her working conditions and duties. These include the introduction of a HAND-type culture. Lorraine picks up the story:

'Suddenly, we have been told that we have to pick up the phone with a "smile in our voices"! How on earth are we meant to do that? In fact, one of my colleagues has actually been disciplined for sounding too miserable on the phone! We also have to smile and appear cheerful to anyone who comes to reception. That sounds OK, but remember the stress that we work under. We are permanently short-staffed and under immense pressure. This forced niceness is just another pressure as far as I am concerned. I have to arrange my face into a fixed smile just to keep management happy.'

Case study 2

Rick works for an international American-style bistro/restaurant in his local town. Part of his training involves learning how to create the HAND-type culture within the restaurant. He says,

'When I first started the job, we were told explicit rules such as we must smile at customers when we greet them, when we take their order, when we bring their drink, when we bring their food, at the end of the meal etc. Even when we bring the bill. We also have to sing "happy birthday" to customers and, of course, smile throughout. It all creates a very happy cheery atmosphere for the customer. Of course, sometimes it's hard work. At the moment I feel great cos I've got a new girlfriend, but sometimes I feel miserable, and being nice can be a real effort.'

DISPLAY RULES

The expectations about which emotions should not be displayed at work in order to create the desired HAND culture have been termed *display rules* by psychologists and these rules (which may be written down formally, or may just be loosely bound up with the culture of the company) tend to specify what kind of emotions may be displayed, for how long and in what way. Thus, for example, flight attendants are expected to feel (or at least *appear* to feel) cheerful and friendly, and show this by smiling during interactions, but not by laughing too heartily nor being so buoyant that customers wonder if they are taking illegal substances. Funeral directors on the other hand are expected to appear sombre and reserved and to show this by *not* smiling – although nor are they expected to be so miserable that they actually cry.

The particular display rules within any one company usually depend on what display rules or expectations are considered normal for the society as a whole – as well as any special rules about the particular profession or organization. As far as the expectations that govern society in general, these can vary according to geographical location. For example, different cultures in the world have different display rules, or expectations about which emotions should and should not be expressed in public. This is illustrated with the example of the case of the opening of the first McDonald's in Moscow, some years ago now. Staff there were trained to smile at customers, as they are in McDonald restaurants throughout the world. However, this particular display rule that 'staff should smile at customers' did not exist in the Moscow culture, and customers were not used to being smiled at by staff. Consequently, the hamburger customers were rather bemused at suddenly being smiled at by cheerful food servers. The customers felt very uncomfortable because they thought that the staff were laughing at them.[7]

Another society where the HAND culture is virtually non-existent and the display rules do not include smiling at customers is Israel. There, smiling at customers is viewed as a sign of inexperience – which is why one customer told an unusually friendly cashier in a supermarket, 'I can tell you are new. No one here smiles or is as friendly as you.'[8] The comparison between the display rule about smiling in Israel and that in America, where most staff are trained to smile at customers, is very obvious to anyone who has experienced both cultures, as another customer in Israel had; she complained to the supermarket cashier that 'in America, all cashiers smile'. The sullen cashier responded with, 'So – go to America!'[9]

One reason that the HAND culture is not as developed in Israel as in other Western countries is that many service employees in Israel are young people who have recently completed compulsory military service and the change from aggressive soldier to polite worker is a difficult transition to make. However, as Israel (like the rest of the world) becomes more and more influenced by the American culture, so the display rules about smiling are changing. For instance, an hotel chain in Eilat (in Israel's Red Sea resort coast) recently introduced an incentive scheme called 'miles of smiles' to encourage staff to smile more[10] and the research that I have conducted in this tiny Middle Eastern country suggests that customers are beginning to expect and demand friendlier service (see later section in this chapter). Certainly I predict that countries where the HAND culture has not yet infiltrated to any great extent (another example is South Africa) will start becoming so within the next decade.

The display rule of smiling that is characteristic of the HAND culture is absent in other cultures too. In the Muslim culture, smiling can be seen as a sign of sexual interest and so it might be felt inappropriate for some women to smile at men, even in a shop situation. In Japan, smiles are seen to convey not friendliness, but an acceptance that the smiler is being corrected or has realized a wrong-doing.[11] In Greece and other Mediterranean countries, however, the display rules about smiling can be even stronger than in America – and this too can leave visitors feeling bemused. One shop-owner commented that German tourists 'cannot believe that we are so friendly; you can see the question on their faces – why are they doing this?'.[10]

Display rules about the expression of *anger* can vary across cultures too. For example, although temper tantrums and violence against parents and adults by children is strongly condemned in America and Britain (and many other countries), the display rule is very different amongst the Yanomano Indians of Brazil. There, children's outbursts are seen as evidence of bravery, so are encouraged.[8]

Even within a culture, however, display rules can vary enormously depending on the profession or organization involved. For example, within the UK or USA, there will tend to be different display rules for service occupations such as shop assistants or flight attendants than for non-service occupations like accountants or scientists. Even within the service industry, there will probably be different rules or expectations for nurses than there are for doctors, for fast-food servers than there are for silver-service personnel, or for discount-store staff and exclusive boutique assistants. Consider the following comments that illustrate these fine distinctions:

'When I go into a cheap chain store, I expect the staff to be young, inexperienced and more interested in gossiping with their friends than in helping me. I know that if I need something in a different size in the changing room, I have to get dressed and go in search of it myself. The staff don't smile – I don't really expect them to. I guess they imagine that they are not being paid to smile. When I go to a store that's a bit more upmarket, though, I expect things to be different. I expect staff to be courteous, friendly and polite. I am paying them to smile!'

'I once needed to see a medical specialist and I waited three months to see one on the National Health Service. The man in question seemed disinterested and distracted. The surroundings

were functional and disordered and I was kept waiting forty-five minutes. The doctor didn't seem to have more than a couple of minutes for me and was very dismissive. I decided to go private and ended up seeing the same man in a plush private clinic. This time, he couldn't be nicer. He got up when I came in, shook my hand, and treated me to the biggest smile. He smiled plenty of times throughout the consultation, which lasted twenty minutes. He shook my hand at the end. I couldn't help thinking that I was paying about ten pounds for each of his smiles.'

DON'T TELL ME TO 'HAVE A NICE DAY'!

'The cashier robotically demands: "Have a nice day!" I foolishly consider this rote-learned request. Did he mean it? Of course not. The beaming youth behind the till doesn't know the first thing about me. His autopilot order oozes all the sincerity of that enraging quip I've heard from a million builders and passersby: "Cheer up, it may never happen." Anything could have happened that morning . . . Someone could have died.'[12]

The above quote reflects the frustration that many of us seem to have with the fake and phony 'Have a Nice Day' culture that is pervading our society as a result of the increasing demand for friendly display rules (why this is increasing is discussed later in this chapter). Over and over again, people I interview complain about the fake and superficial nature of this culture, and they really seem to lament the loss of honest, down-to-earth expression of feeling. This backlash against the fake, plasticky HAND culture is reflected in a British comedienne's comment about Prime Minister Tony Blair. She says of him, 'He just seems so plastic and I'd like to know what's behind that clean cut, smiley image'.[13] Certainly, his ability to appear emotional at times when previous British Prime Ministers might have appeared cool and emotionless has led some critics to suspect that he is faking the emotion. For instance, one person I interviewed said,

'Tony Blair is either a very sensitive soul, or a great actor. There are tears in his eyes whenever he talks of a national disaster. He cried at Yad Vashesm, the Holocaust Memorial in Jerusalem. His voice broke when he sent condolences to Germany over their tragic rail accident recently.'

This ability to express emotions that are appropriate to the prevailing circumstances is criticized because it appears fake and being fake would appear to be one of the modern crimes of our society. Consider the comment of one source who points out that 'synthetic compassion can be more offensive than none at all'.[14] Would we really all prefer others to show compassion only if they really meant it? Would we really prefer Tony Blair or Bill Clinton to send cold messages of condolence to bereaved families?

Perhaps these are extreme cases, and we would be better off looking to more mundane situations to see if people really dislike the fake sentiments encapsulated in the demand to 'have a nice day'. At least one researcher insists that we do strongly dislike the HAND culture that we live in; customers, she says, 'frequently have negative reactions towards what they believe to be "phony smiles"[7]'.[8] This is summed up in the following quote that appeared in a British newspaper (and that always amuses American audiences):

> 'Genuine friendliness is fine, but not the insincere, oily charm we have imported from America. Receptionists ooze it when they welcome you in patronizing sing-song voices. Salespeople employ it all the time . . . while bank counter staff are trained to greet you so fondly that you have to peer through the bullet-proof glass to check it's not an ex-lover counting out your cash!'[15]

This dislike of false friendliness does not seem to be restricted to the UK. In the movie *Falling Down* when Michael Douglas's character Defense objects to being expected to call servers in a fast-food diner by their first names as displayed on their name badges, he says, 'Why should I call you Ralph and Sheila? I don't want to be your buddies, I just want some breakfast.' (Although, as he then proceeds to use a machine gun in order to obtain his breakfast, it is possible that Defense does not represent the average American!)

Can it really be that we dislike the HAND culture so much that we prefer the culture more typically associated with the average New York cab driver? Do we really want a return to the days when 'customer service' was characterized by grunts and scowls? To find out, I conducted some interviews and, when faced with the stark choice between fake niceness and downright rudeness, the niceties invariably won. Comments include:

'I'd rather people in shops or restaurants were friendly towards me than miserable. I hate rudeness, and would rather shop somewhere else than in a place where the staff are rude.'

'There is an excellent restaurant in North London where the food is great . . . but the staff so rude, that I refuse to go there any more. The last time I went and I wanted to pay by credit card. The meal I'd had was very reasonable value – a meal deal thing. The owner scowled at my card and snarled that he was hardly making any-thing on the meal as it was so the least I could do was offer cash! I'd rather take my custom where it's appreciated.'

'I have two sandwich bars within walking distance of my office. One is cheaper and nearer, but the staff are sullen and miserable. They act like I am being a pain by just walking in and wanting food. The other place is more expensive, further away, and, if I'm hon-est, not really as good in terms of the variety. But the staff are so welcoming and friendly! They know my name and how I prefer my sandwich without butter. You can guess where I go!'

Clearly, customers want staff to be warm and friendly, and this is shown not just in the above quotes, but in a survey I have carried out in four different countries.[16,17,18,19,20] I asked 100 students in each country (United Kingdom, United States, Australia and Israel) how much, on a scale of 1–8, they wanted and expected warm and friendly service from service personnel such as shop assistants, bank clerks, fast-food servers and supermarket clerks. The lower the score (eg 1), the more they wanted warm, friendly service.

Over 70 per cent of respondents in each of the countries scored 1, 2 or 3, indicating that they wanted this 'Have a Nice Day'-ness a great deal. The country that seemed to expect the HAND culture the most was the UK (84 per cent of people scored 1–3) with the least from Australia (73 per cent).

It would seem then that, contrary to some popular opinion, we do want and expect the HAND culture in at least three major Western soci-eties (and one Middle Eastern). We want employees whom we encounter in the service industry to be nice to us. This is perhaps not too surprising – we might expect that we would prefer people to be nice to us than rude. But the HAND culture is about more than niceness – it is primarily concerned with *false* niceness. So, the more interesting question to ask would be, 'Do we want shop assistants etc to be nice to us, *even if it means they are faking it*?' In other words, maybe we all want warm friendly service staff, but only if they genuinely feel like being warm and friendly? Not according to my survey!

A substantial percentage of the people I asked in each country want the forced *bonhomie*, the fake smiles and the phony grins that typify the HAND culture. Of the people surveyed, 57 per cent of Britons and 56 per cent of Australians reported being quite happy if the smiles and warmth from service personnel are faked. (Scores of 1, 2 or 3.)

The figures are surprisingly higher in Israel and America – 76 per cent of Israelis surveyed and 63 per cent of Americans are happy to tolerate phoniness from service personnel.

This does still mean, of course, that around 40 per cent of Brits, Australians and Americans will not tolerate phoniness. That means that more than one in three of us are likely to dislike the HAND culture. These are the people likely to scream an enraged 'Don't tell me to have a nice day!'

Unfortunately for those of us whose job it is to maintain a HAND culture, society tends to pander to the majority, which means that the chances of the HAND culture slipping quietly away are unlikely. However, I do think that the culture will evolve into a more sophisticated version. What is likely to happen is that the silent minority who dislike the fake smiles are going to grow into a much noisier majority and start demanding a reduction in faking. Managers will have to take notice and I predict a future where superficial smiles and throwaway greetings will be replaced by sincere smiles and depth of feeling as demanded by a society increasingly irritated by the sugary charms of the HAND culture. Society will, I believe, become less scripted and more responsive – in fact, in my view, it is those service companies that are able to move in this direction that will gain a real competitive edge in the new millennium.

The only problem with this scenario is, how on earth can we ensure that employees are able to give more genuine responses? After all, we are slipping into scripted cultures precisely because customers want the smiles – and employees can only give them day after day in an often insincere way. It is almost impossible to genuinely feel each and every emotion we are expected to display (more is said about this in later chapters). How is this transition from feigning to feeling to happen? We will return to this intriguing question in the next chapter.

Meanwhile, back to my survey. What is puzzling about my findings is that Israelis, who have perhaps the least strong HAND-type culture of the four countries I surveyed, had the highest tolerance towards phony displays. What should this be? Perhaps, because the Israelis are so unused to the HAND culture, they would never expect shop assistants to genuinely care or be genuinely friendly. Introduction of the HAND culture is still in its early stages in Israel and, although it is obviously seen (at least according to my findings) as a welcome change, there may still be some (understandable) disbelief that service personnel can display genuine smiles and friendliness.

DOES THE HAND CULTURE EXIST OUTSIDE THE SERVICE INDUSTRY?

So far, I have talked about the HAND culture as being something that people in customer service jobs such as shop assistants, receptionists, telephone operators, bank clerks etc create in order to have a friendly atmosphere for customers. Certainly, it has been thought for many years now that emotional control by employers is something peculiar to service-type jobs and that if you were in a job that did not demand contact with customers, you were pretty free to express whatever emotion you were feeling as and when you felt it. There are sound reasons why appropriate display of emotion has been more pertinent to the frontline. Employees who deal with the customers of an organization 'represent the corporation's frontline to customers and embody the image that the organization wants to project'.[21] These employees are naturally encouraged by management to 'project an air of pleasant hospitality and to conceal any negative feelings they may have behind a benevolent facial expression'.[22] This may involve becoming what one source calls a 'one-minute friend'[23] and although employees in the service industry may 'not particularly feel like being cordial and becoming a one-minute friend to the next customer who approaches, this is indeed what frontline work entails'.[23] The emphasis in the service industry is on the transient relationship of the server to the customer; the server has about a minute to project the caring emotions that most friendships take a lifetime to genuinely accumulate. Is it any wonder that these emotions are often likely to be faked?

The HAND culture within the service industry is, I believe, likely to become more and more commonplace, not less. This is because, increasingly, the emotional style of offering the service is 'part of the service itself'.[2] That is, no longer is a service transaction simply about providing an airline seat, a hamburger, a new car or whatever. The way in which the seat, car or burger is offered and the emotions that the offerer displays are as much as a part of the service as the handing over of the product. The reason that this is becoming more and more the case in today's society, and is likely to become even more so in tomorrow's society, is that over the last decade there has been a proliferation of the service industry offering very similar products within an increasingly competitive market. This has tended to result in an evening out of many of the differences in price and quality between those services so that, overall, one hamburger is pretty similar to another, one hotel room the same as the next and one airline seat little different from that of its rival.[24] The only way that companies who offer similar products can stand out from the crowd is by offering a superior quality of *service*, and this refers not to the physical nature of the service, but its psychological nature. That is, it is not in the aftercare, delivery of product, style of ticket etc that companies can distinguish themselves any more, but in the emotional way they can make customers feel. By being nice, friendly and warm, service employees make customers feel good and thus they are more likely to return for future purchases. This will be returned to in chapter 5.

Thus, the really competitive company will be more keen than ever to ensure its employees adopt and maintain the HAND culture. This may be good news for the customer (at least for those who don't mind if the smiles are fake) but can be bad news for the employee, as we will discover in chapter 7. But what may be really startling is that people whose jobs are not 'customer-facing' may still have to maintain a HAND culture. For the HAND culture is starting to pervade jobs and job roles well away from 'customer-facing' jobs. There are a number of reasons for this:

1. In today's increasingly insecure world, where competition is stiffer and stiffer for fewer and fewer jobs and where 'downsizing' and 'delayering' are part of everyday language, workers are beginning to cotton on to the fact that it is no longer enough just to be good at your work. More and more, workers are expected to be enthusiastic, team players and excited by their jobs and the company. This requires display of certain HAND-type emotions such as enthusiasm and interest even away from customers – and these emotions may or may not be genuinely felt (see chapter 6 for more on this). This can have negative consequences for the employee and the organization, as disagreements are suppressed and anger and negative emotions that do not fit the HAND

culture are hidden. The evidence for this is presented in chapter 6, but even the simple finding that seven out of ten Americans are now afraid to question their superiors[25] provides strong support. They are reluctant to speak out these days, even if they know that their superiors are wrong and speaking out could prevent the company making an expensive mistake. To speak out, to complain or to appear negative could jeopardize the impression we need to create of being a happy worker. After all, managers are still likely to believe that a happy worker is a productive one. This is illustrated by David's experience:

> 'I work in computer maintenance in a company that is going through a real cost-cutting exercise. Just the other day the company laid off fifty-five staff and this has happened three times in the two years I have been here. I feel like I am walking on eggshells at work, always afraid that if I say or do anything wrong, I will be the next one out. I always pretend to be cheerful and enthusiastic – it always seems to be the moaners who are made redundant. The problem is that I don't know what to do if I spot a mistake from my boss, which I occasionally do. If I point it out, he may not like my doing so. If I don't we will end up having to recall a huge volume of product. Sometimes I don't say anything – it's more risk to me to speak out than not.'

A dramatic example of the reluctance employees have in challenging their boss is demonstrated by the case of a flight in 1978 in Portland, Oregon. The airline pilot was a domineering boss whose co-pilots were afraid of him. As the flight came in to land, the pilot noticed a problem with the landing gear and began circling the airfield whilst he ordered his co-pilots to try and sort the problem out. Meanwhile the co-pilots became aware of a rather more serious problem – they were running out of fuel! They tried to tell their boss, but were dismissed by him. Afraid for their job prospects, afraid to speak out, they kept quiet. The plane crashed, killing ten people.[25]

2. The other reason for the increased prevalence of the HAND culture outside of customer-facing jobs is that in the 'old days' there was a clear line between customers and suppliers, but now that line is rather fuzzy. The growth of internal marketplaces where departments or branches within a company are expected to compete with those outside the company mean that the term 'customer' applies to a wider range of people.

Stakeholders, suppliers and clients are all customers and thus there are few jobs any more that are not at all 'customer-facing'.

This is illustrated by the comments of a waitress in a bar who said;

> 'The waitresses have to be nice to the bartenders because we need our drinks fast. The bartenders have to be nice to us because if our customers complain it is his fault. The cooks . . . have to be nice to the waitresses to get the secret drinks we bring them from the bar.'[26]

Here, the workers in the various departments have to keep in with each other in order that they can obtain what they need. This is not so very different from the customer–employee relationship, in that maintaining good relationships means having to at least feign friendliness.

Another job role away from the customer that increasingly requires a HAND-type culture is what is called the *boundary* role. This is the person who sits on the boundary between one department and another, or one branch and another. For instance, the secretary or personal assistant in one department may never have to deal with a customer, but is expected to be warm and pleasant in all his or her dealings with other departments, Head Office, or suppliers. Kate illustrates this by discussing her own role:

> 'I work as secretary for a professor and I rarely deal with any actual customers – in our case, the students. I am more likely to deal with other professors, with university management, with other academic departments or with in-house suppliers such as catering or reprographic departments. In all cases, I am expected to be cheerful and friendly, even when they are demanding to speak to the professor when she's not there, or when the expected meal for an important business meeting has not materialized.'

So, the feeling is that the HAND culture is no longer restricted to people who work in customer-facing jobs. More and more of us are going to have to maintain and put up with this culture in our day-to-day jobs. When I was carrying out my survey in the four different countries into the expectations that people have of the HAND culture, I wondered what people actually thought about this culture in offices, away from the frontline. Do people actually want the HAND culture from people they work with – colleagues, peers, subordinates and bosses – as well as people who serve them in the service industry? Surely it is more understandable that we should tolerate faked warmth from shop servers in their fleeting interactions with us, than from our colleagues who we spend about seven hours a day with?

I asked the same people the same questions as before – but this time I wanted to know what they thought in the context of people they work with. First of all, do people actually want the warm, friendly emotions characteristic of the HAND culture from colleagues, the boss or subordinates?

I found that the British want warm, friendly emotions *per se* less from people they work with than from people who serve them in the service industry. They still want and expect them a great deal and the percentages wanting these friendly displays are still well over 60 per cent. However, the Brits clearly expect warmth more from service personnel than they do from those people they work with.

The Australians and Americans, however, were slightly different. They were more likely to expect these warm friendly displays from people they work with than from people who serve them in the service industry! That is, they were more likely to expect their colleagues, boss or subordinates to be nice to them than the store assistant who serves them their lunchtime sandwich. As far as the Israeli sample were concerned, similar percentages of respondents expected warm display from both colleagues at work and service personnel.

What does this mean? Why should the Brits alone expect more warmth from people they encounter fleetingly than people they work with on an on-going basis? Although the average differences between the service and non-service expectations is not huge, it still suggests that there may be some cultural display rule that is different in the UK than in the other countries I looked at. It could be that in Britain, there is a much stronger 'smiley' display rule amongst service industry workers than there is amongst colleagues. Perhaps there is an expectation that there is less need to smile and be friendly all the time with colleagues with whom longer-term relationships can be built than there is with service personnel who must become 'one-minute friends' in every interaction. This is illustrated in the following comments from two participants in the study:

'I do expect shop assistants to be nice and friendly towards me. They are being paid for that – by me. Part of what I pay for the product goes to the shop assistant – I am paying their salary, so

they should jolly well be nice to me! At work, it's different. There, my colleagues are being paid to do a job just like me. They are not paid to be nice to me and nor am I paid to be nice to them. But it is still important to develop good relations over time, so we invariably are nice to each other. I just wouldn't expect them to say "have a nice day" every five minutes or to smile at me all the time.'

'I want everyone to be nice! It makes the world a nicer place. But, at work, there are many different ways that colleagues etc can be "nice" – other than just saying meaningless nice words. They can do favours, share treats, do something nice. A shop assistant can't really do that – they don't have the time. The only way they can convey niceness is in a smile or something.'

Thus, whilst it is still important to the Brits that their work colleagues are nice to them, they may expect this 'niceness' to be manifested in less superficial ways than the simple smiles or greetings that service personnel use to be 'nice'.

The opposite could be true in the other countries; there may be an expectation there that it is more important to be nice and friendly to people with whom there are long-term relationships than for the 'one-minute friends' in service interactions. For instance, one Israeli told me:

'Why should I expect people I don't know to be nice to me if I don't expect it from people I do know? I don't care whether the shop assistant likes me or not – I'll never see them again. But I have to work with my colleagues all the time, so we have to be nice to each other.'

Before we can address this conundrum effectively, let us look at the second question in the survey which was concerned with the expectation that the warm, friendly emotions are actually *genuine*, rather than faked. The results show that, for all the countries, there is a dramatically higher expectation that warm emotions from colleagues are genuine than there is from service personnel. In other words, we are all much more tolerant of faked emotional display from service personnel than we are from our colleagues at work.

The lesson to be learned here is this. If you work in an office with colleagues, you are well advised to be warm and friendly – but make sure that your displays appear genuine! If, on the other hand, you work in the service industry, you should still be warm and friendly, but you don't need to worry too much about your displays appearing genuine. Most people are more tolerant of phoniness in the service industry – in fact, the results here suggest that they even expect it. Of course, this does not mean that this is the ideal situation, since the best service employees are still the ones that either smile because they mean it, or can make their smiles appear like they mean it! I'll be showing you how you can achieve both these states later in the book.

What the research I have presented here clearly shows is that the 'Have a Nice Day' culture is here to stay and I have suggested throughout this chapter that it is likely to become even more prevalent in more companies and in more countries as we head into the next millennium. This is both good and bad. It is good for those of us that like the phony displays, and it is obviously good for business as will be shown in chapter 6. But the problem is that faking emotions that are required as part of the 'Have a Nice Day' culture can be unhealthy and can lead to a series of symptoms that I have termed the 'Have a Nice Day' syndrome. This will be discussed in detail in chapter 7. In the meantime, the next chapter takes a closer look at the various types of scripted cultures that we are becoming increasingly familiar with in our society.

Chapter 3

'Have A Rotten Day!' – And Other Scripted Cultures

'I'm sure I'm not alone, when ringing any organization, in not wanting to be greeted by a theatre script'[1]

The journalist who made this comment is not alone. According to my research (see chapter 2), at least 40 per cent of us do not want to be greeted by the fake and phony sentiments that the 'theatre script' in the above quote refers to. However, the vast majority of us *do* want warm and friendly smiles, and managers and organizations in much of Western society seem to have latched onto *this* finding, whilst being oblivious of our dislike of phoniness. In other words, over the last decade or so, companies have been so keen to give us smiles in order that their company can be the most 'smiley' company of all that they have jointly created a scripted society. Their efforts to be seen as the cosiest, most friendly airline company, supermarket, hamburger joint or whatever may actually backfire as they become known instead as the most scripted company with the phoniest smiles. Consider these comments from people I have interviewed:

'You know how it is – you ring up an hotel to make a booking, and they launch into their routine. They have to tell you who they are, who you have called and that they would like to help you! I expect them to want to help me – that is why I'm ringing! Who cares who they are? What do I care if it's Tracey or Karen who takes my call? I usually forget their name immediately anyway. Meanwhile, it's costing me money to listen to their spiel – if I am calling overseas, this can be very irritating indeed.'

'When I worked in an ice-cream parlour, we were actually given a written script to tell us what to say to customers! We had to smile,

say hello, ask them how they are today, smile again, ask what they would like and so on. Like we don't have minds! Actually, after three weeks of following the script, you don't have a mind any more – you go on automaton and you stop listening and responding. You just recite your lines like a robot. Is this what the customer wants?'

'You can tell when someone doesn't mean the smile or the words are just part of the script. I always like to unscript people by making them smile genuinely or getting them to say something that goes outside their script. Asking them if they've had a hard day usually gets through to the person behind the script – it humanizes them.'

Scripted cultures are not necessarily 'Have a Nice Day' cultures. Most companies, especially in the service industry, are frantically foisting this culture on their staff and customers, but some organizations, because of the nature of their business, are still adopting the 'Have a Rotten Day' script and this will be discussed later in this chapter. There is also a third kind of culture, what I call the 'Have a Cool Day' script, that is adopted by those companies that want to appear cool and emotionless to their customers – this too will be examined later in this chapter.

But first, let us return to the most popular script of all, the one that is likely to take over and infiltrate much of the working world, the script that goes hand in hand with the 'Have a Nice Day' culture. This script I call the 'fast-food server' script, because it has been long associated with certain American fast-food restaurants that were credited with introducing the standardized greetings across all its outlets – indeed, this is why one author calls this influence the 'McDonaldization of society'.[2]

THE 'FAST-FOOD SERVER' SCRIPT

Workers who are most likely to adopt the 'fast-food server' script include the following:

- Fast-food servers
- Shop assistants
- Waiters/waitresses

- Receptionists

- Flight attendants

This script, which is the most prominent feature of the 'Have a Nice Day' culture, is characterized by:

- Wide smiles

- Phrases learned by rote

- Clichéd greetings

- Long-winded introductions

- Inability to cope with unusual requests

The 'fast-food server' script is the most popular one in Western society and, as discussed in chapter 2, is likely to become a more and more prominent feature of our world. There is a very good reason for this. Customers, as my own research has shown, want staff to be nice to them. They will pay more for friendly service. They will return to the friendly store. Being nice pays. As one researcher said, 'The company's profit rides on a smiling face'.[3] And, in order to ensure that their staff are nice at all times – even when they don't feel like being nice – employers prepare scripts to tell them how to behave, when to smile, how to act etc. For example, at McDonald's, fast-food workers are told to be 'cheerful and polite at all times' and crew people are 'often reprimanded for not smiling'.[4] At Tupperware, the home-party plastic-ware company, 'good cheer is virtually mandated',[5] whilst at Disneyland and DisneyWorld, recruits are trained to 'wish every guest a pleasant day' and to 'say "thank you" as you herd them through the gate'.[5] Supermarket trainees in one firm were told that 'a friendly smile is a must'[6] and even a firm offering temporary jobs to backpackers in Australia advises that 'a happy, bright, smiling face' is required.[7]

And, the script works. It does ensure that staff create the required HAND culture – as demonstrated by one waiter who said, 'I always smile at them . . . that's part of my uniform'.[8] Being nice to customers instils a sense of well-being, goodwill or satisfaction and if the use of scripts ensures that staff consider smiles as part of their uniform, then the technique must be considered successful. In fact, if a company is successful in ensuring that its employees follow the 'fast-food server' script, then they have powerful ammunition to encourage more cus-tomers to use their services. Consider this full-page advertisement for Southwest Airlines that appeared in *USA Today*, 28 April 1998:

'Airplanes don't smile . . . and you'll never hear a runway say "Have a nice day". Great airlines are made up of great people.'

This airline is selling itself entirely on the HAND culture that its staff cre-ate. The ad is saying that the most important aspect of their service is their staff who, unlike physical objects like aeroplanes or runways, can smile and say 'have a nice day'! In other words, the people can follow the script, whereas the planes cannot and so the planes become almost incidental to Southwest Airlines' advertising strategy. This is increas-ingly common amongst airlines (more examples are given elsewhere in this book) and the reason is that the physical aspects of air transporta-tion are very similar from one airline to another and are often beyond the direct control of the airline anyway. That is, the size of the seats is dictated by cost implications and safety regulations. The comfort and extra facilities on offer are also dictated by cost and mean that compa-nies cannot offer much extra and still remain competitive, at least within the economy-class sector. Even the safety record, which might be considered to be the most important customer consideration when choosing an airline, cannot be easily advertised since most airlines have suffered some loss and no one wants to 'tempt fate' by bragging about an outstanding safety record. All that is really left is the emotional style of the employees. Airlines can introduce 'fast-food server' scripts at little apparent cost (but see chapter 7 for some indication of the real, hidden cost) and create the 'Have a Nice Day' culture that will attract customers.

THE 'LAWYER' SCRIPT

A far less common script is adopted in the 'Have a Cool Day' cultures. In these cases, warm and friendly emotional displays are not appropri-ate and the display rules call for cool, aloof and emotionless displays. The 'lawyer' script is characterized by:

- No smiles

- Lack of warmth

- No laughter or tears

- Emotionless face

It is not just lawyers, who must be objective and neutral, who adopt this script. The 'Have a Cool Day' culture is an important part of many work (and social) settings, as the following comments illustrate:

> 'If you are working in an emergency room and a mother rushes in with a badly mangled child, you can't show your distress, even if you know that the child is in terrible pain and has little chance to survive. You have to hold your own feelings.'   Nurse[9]

> 'Wheelchair users . . . expressly mask their own emotions so as to manage others'. They cover their embarrassment with good humor . . . they hide resentment behind calm graciousness . . . even when [they] feel justified in their emotional reactions, their public expression often sharply contrasts with their private feelings.'   Wheelchair user[10]

> 'In my business, you repress these feelings, you learn not to show emotions, especially anger. It's unpriestly.'
>   Priest talking about being passed over for promotion[11]

The focus of the 'lawyer' script, then, is in *masking* emotions, hiding what is felt – but not faking what is not felt. Workers who must follow this script have only to concentrate on hiding their feelings, whilst workers following the 'fast-food server' script may have both to hide what they really feel and fake what they do not feel. It could be harder mental work to have both to hide and fake (this will be discussed in more detail in chapter 7), but, on the other hand, the felt emotions that must be hidden in the 'Have a Cool Day' culture may be far more intense. The following case studies demonstrate this point:

Case study 1
Andrew is a doctor working in Accident and Emergency, or ER. He continually has to manage or control his emotions at work and says:
   'From the minute I go to work, I have to hide what I really feel and fake what I don't feel. I have to pretend to be interested in the little aches and pains of my patients on the ward-rounds. I have to listen to parents and relatives and feign interest and concern. But the hardest

for me is when I have to hide my real raw emotions when, say, a patient dies or a child is badly injured. I always care, even after three years in the job. When I have to tell a relative that their loved one isn't going to make it – that's when I have to work hard at suppressing my own feelings.'

Case study 2

Jayne is a barrister and tends to work in a very poised and calm manner both in and out of the courtroom. She says:

'I am very rational at work and never let my emotions cloud my rational thought processes. We are trained this way – there is a certain demeanour that most lawyers adopt. In court, whatever happens, I am able to present a mask of cool, calm – even if inside I am panicking or wondering what on earth will happen. I once had a client accused of shoplifting. It was her first offence – she was a mother of two and had just lost her own mother when the offence happened. She said that she just forgot to pay – she was so distracted that she just walked out of the store. I was convinced that she was telling the truth and was sure she would be believed. Anyway, it was a first offence, she had two small children, so the chances of her being sent down were remote. But she was sentenced to six months in prison, and she was just horrified and started screaming and crying. I felt terrible too and it was a real struggle to maintain my poised mask whilst I went through the legal bits and bobs with the judge. So, not all lawyers are emotionless – we just wear that mask for work.'

Those workers for whom the 'lawyer' script is likely to be especially relevant include the following:

- Lawyers/attorneys
- Doctors
- Nurses
- Some managers
- Politicians

Thus, whilst the 'fast-food server' script tends to characterize the service industry, the 'lawyer' script is more common elsewhere. Whilst the 'fast-food server' script is used to make other people feel good, the 'lawyer' script may be used to assert authority, superiority or merely to convey a mask of professionalism. Some managers attempt to assert their authority by being cool and emotionless. Indeed, one source claimed that many middle managers have expectations that their job involves the ability to 'exercise iron self-control and to have the ability to mask all emotion behind bland, smiling, agreeable public faces'.[12] We tend to associate authority in this society with an unemotional persona, so this 'affective neutrality' reinforces the power that the managers have and helps keep their subordinates from challenging them.[13]

Other workers use the 'lawyer' script to conform to a display rule called 'detached concern'. This means displaying enough concern to show that you care, but little enough to remain professional and uninvolved. Thus, members of the medical profession try to create the impression that they are sufficiently detached or objective to make sound medical decisions without being clouded by their feelings – yet concerned enough to create the impression that their decisions are based on caring understanding. As one doctor who works in Accident and Emergency (ER) said:

'I cannot get emotionally involved in every case – I would be an emotional wreck at the end of each day. I try and remain emotionally detached. Anyway, we don't always make the best decisions when we feel emotional. Sometimes we have to make cool rational decisions based on the evidence available. For instance, in resuscitation, there reaches a point when it is not rational to carry on any longer. If I was emotionally involved, I could never reach that point. Even though we try and stay cool and rational, we still have to show care and empathy to families. I may have coolly ordered the stopping of resus, then go out and tell the family how terribly sorry I am and how we did all we could. It is not lying, but the emotions that I detached myself from in the resus room must be displayed in the right way in the family room.'

This preoccupation among some professional groups with emotionless masks reflects the negative views that we as a society have about emotions in general, as discussed in chapter 1. We tend to associate cool, rational processes with lack of strong emotion and so we like to think that those people whose decisions may affect our lives (such as doctors, nurses and politicians) should be emotionally neutral. This is one reason that many societies get so upset by the sexual liaisons of their politicians. The feeling is that if a politician cannot control his sexual feelings, then how can he (and it usually is a 'he') make important state decisions without his judgement being clouded by other emotions?

THE 'DEBT COLLECTOR' SCRIPT

'They pay me to be mean.'   Police Interrogator[14]

This script is the total opposite of the 'fast-food server' script and is often used in those rare 'Have a Rotten Day' cultures. Of course, we have all encountered shops and companies where the 'Have a Rotten Day' culture appears to be prevail, but this culture is rarely intentionally maintained. For instance, this anecdote illustrates this culture in a large nationalized postal company in the UK that, by all accounts, does not deliberately attempt to foster it:

> *'I needed a tax disc for my car and whenever I have to renew my disc, I have to travel twenty minutes in the car during the working day to my nearest main post office. Why I can't get the disc at my local post office, I don't know. Anyway, I went and queued for twenty minutes and finally reached the front desk. I produced all the documentation, only to be told, somewhat gleefully, that I had brought my insurance schedule instead of the certificate. I was pretty upset and fed up – I was late for work and would not be able to return. The counter staff's attitude was "tough". She just didn't even pretend to care. If I had any choice, I would not have returned to that post office.'*

This is exactly the aim of the 'debt collector' script or the 'Have a Rotten Day' culture. Employees in this culture do not want customers to return. This is why, as a culture, it is rarely deliberately adopted as company policy (although individual workers may adopt it in order to have an easier and less busy day at work), and there are very few types of job that would routinely use the 'debt collector' script. Those that do, include:

- Debt or bill collectors
- Club bouncers
- Security personnel
- Police officers

These workers adopt the 'debt collector' script specifically because the organization wants to discourage re-use of the service. Thus, debt collectors want to discourage continued debt, bouncers and security personnel want to discourage inappropriate approaches whilst police officers want to discourage re-offending. The 'Have a Rotten Day' culture promotes mistrust, hostility, irritation or bad will towards others in order to instil unease, fear or worry. By displaying emotions such as anger, irritation or disapproval, these workers can induce anxiety in the target of their displays. This anxiety can be reduced by complying with the demands or expectations of the worker. Thus, the suspect can confess in order to reduce the hostility displayed by the police interrogator, the debtor can pay his or her bill in order to reduce the anger displayed by the bill collector, and the would-be trouble-maker can go elsewhere in order to reduce the wrath of the bouncer.

I should point out here that there are many workers whose jobs require them to flit from one script to another. Most of the professions that I have mentioned tend to conform to the particular set of display rules bound up in the specific script enforced by the culture. Some workers, however, even within these cultures, are required to be flexible and change their emotional display according to the circumstance. For instance, debt collectors can switch from one script to another; a researcher who trained as a debt collector was told that he should display warmth and concern ('fast-food server' script) to anxious debtors or those whose debts were not so old, irritation or anger ('debt collector' script) to indifferent debtors or those with old mounting debts, and calmness and neutrality ('lawyer' script) to angry debtors.[15]

Another example of switching scripts is in the case of a team of nurses who were expected to present an emotionally flat demeanour ('lawyer' script) in the operating room, to be warm and friendly ('fast-food server' script) when talking to patients and their families and to let their real feelings of rage or disgust ('debt collector' script) out during breaks or in informal meetings with colleagues.[6]

Police officers, too, are frequently required to switch scripts according to circumstance. For instance, in a study of police detectives in America,[16] researchers found that officers were expected to sometimes be nice and sometimes be nasty. They were expected to adopt 'fast-food server' scripts with victims of crimes, by being pleasant and sympathetic, whilst then becoming mean and nasty with the 'debt collector' script with suspected criminals. Sometimes, even with a suspected criminal, an officer may switch from being warm and friendly to being threatening and hostile. This routine, known as 'good cop/bad cop', is more commonly adopted by two officers who take it in turns to play out each role. The idea is that the criminal should feel afraid of the 'bad cop' but reassured by the 'good cop', who offers to protect him from his aggressive partner – in return for a full confession. The good cop/bad cop routine is used frequently in many aspects of everyday life, as the following case study demonstrates:

Case study

'My husband and I often use the good cop/bad cop routine when we have cause to complain about service in a restaurant or hotel. He plays the baddie role, and gets aggressive and threatening, whilst I play the nice guy who tries to calm my husband down whilst suggesting things that might appease him. For instance, we were once staying in an hotel in San Diego. We were woken up at five am by a security guard knocking on our door to deliver a fax. We were furious to be woken for it at such a time and in the morning we went to the reception to complain. My husband started to make a fuss, in a loud voice and getting very angry. I visibly tried to calm him down and explained to the manager that he was very angry and perhaps a reduction in our bill would be a sensible move. We, quite rightly, were given the night free.'

TECHNIQUES FOR STICKING TO THE SCRIPT

> *'How do I control my feelings when I have to give bad news like firing someone? How do I mask how I am really feeling so there is no leakage?'* Manager

Since the three kinds of scripts that I have discussed above are likely to govern so many jobs to some extent (especially the 'fast-food server' script), how can we ensure that we meet the demands of our employer or customer (or even colleagues) at all times? 'Sticking to the script' is not just about learning your lines and reciting them by rote. It is much more about *emotion management* than it is about just reciting some well-learned lines.

Emotion management is the effort in creating a particular emotional display that is appropriate to the circumstance. We perform emotion management not only throughout our working day but also in our social interactions. Consider these examples of emotion management in everyday life:

- Pretending to be interested in your spouse's problems when all you want to do is have a relaxing hot bath.

- Meeting an old friend in the street and pretending to be interested in his or her life.

- Pretending to be stern and angry as you tell your kids off, when really you just want to laugh.

- Holding your anger in as you deal with unhelpful staff.

- Concealing your irritation at your friend's snide comments.

- Suppressing your impatience with your relative's slow driving.

- Praising your mother's new but unflattering haircut.

- Hiding jealousy on hearing of your friend's promotion.

- Pretending to be thrilled with your neighbour's new Rottweiler.

We manage our emotions in a number of different ways that we learn as we grow from children to adults. (Children are notoriously poor at emotion management and are often embarrassingly honest!) The ways in which we exercise emotional control include:

Facial expressions
We arrange our faces into expected emotional expressions such as smiles or frowns. This is the most obvious way in which we can attempt to control our emotions and is the method most widely used. It is very easy to plaster a smile on your face, or to look sad or concerned. However, poor attention to facial expression can result in the emotional control being seen for what it is – deliberate attempts to manipulate your emotional expression. The best way to make your emotion management more convincing is to pay attention to other areas of emotional control too.

Lips and eyes
We pay special attention to our lips and eyes, which are at the heart of emotional expression. This is why some people maintain that it is only genuine smiles that reach the eyes. Thus, it is the combination of arranging your lips *and* eyes into the required emotion that can help make the emotional display appear convincing.

Voice

Our tone of voice and the intonation we use reveals a lot about how we feel, so we should pay attention to this aspect when we are controlling our emotions. Consider an example in an old episode of the popular American sitcom, *Friends*. Joey, the aspiring actor, has appeared in a rather bad play, but tells his friends that he has been spotted by a talent scout. Phoebe exclaims incredulously, 'From seeing you in this play?!' Seeing the downcast reaction of Joey, she immediately controls her emotion of incredulity and repeats the phrase using different intonation: 'From seeing you in this play!' This time, her tone of voice is saying, 'Of course you've been spotted from this play!' and thus she attempts (rather belatedly) to keep her real feelings hidden.

Body language

Our body language too can reveal a lot about how we are feeling. Crossed arms can indicate boredom, hands on the hips aggression, whilst hands behind the head can indicate arrogance. Body language is often the one area that we pay less attention to when we are trying to control our emotional displays and thus, psychologists and other body language experts can often tell how someone is really feeling by their body language. So, one way to really improve your emotion management skills would be to make more effort to ensure that your body language accurately reflects the emotion you want to convey, rather than the emotion you actually feel.

'Neutralizing' emotion

This is a clever technique that can be used not only to manage and control your own emotion, but also that of other people. This is particularly useful when someone, whether it be a customer, client or colleague, displays strong emotions such as anger. How should we deal with angry people? The natural response to someone else's anger is to become angry yourself. However, the better response that will produce the most effective result is to hide your own anger and use the 'neutralizing' technique to manage the anger of the other person.

This technique is especially useful for employees who work in the service industry where there are often display rules that prevent the expression of anger by employees towards customers. By neutralizing the anger of the customer, the situation can be diffused. The technique can be summed up in the words of one shop worker who gives this advice on calming angry customers:

'If you talk softer and softer, they're going to have to stop to listen or they're not going to hear anything you're saying. The louder you get, the louder they get. And if you start to tone it down, they start to tone it down.'[15]

Thus, the angrier the customer gets, the calmer you should get. This is a very effective emotion management technique. Try it!

'Buffering' emotion

This technique is more often used by organizations than by individuals. It consists of a set of procedures whose aim it is to *compartmentalize* emotion. The goal is to keep the emotional situation in one part of the organization, or at least away from other more sensitive areas of the company. For instance, personal assistants or customer-service personnel tend to deal with the more emotionally charged situations whilst the 'backstage' personnel can perform their work without the emotional demands of the public. This means that it is the customer service representative who is the target of your anger, not the CEO (who should really be the target) who is protected from such emotional outpouring. In this way, the emotion is managed or controlled.

Other examples of emotional buffering as an emotion management technique include companies that have public relations officers to deal with the emotional public and press when a crisis occurs in their company (for instance, if a plane were to crash, it is usually the PR person who bears the brunt of rage against the company, not the CEO), pop stars who have bodyguards and personal assistants to control the strong emotions of the fans, and even ordinary workers who have been known to pretend to be out of the office when an irate client calls so that their colleague deals with the emotion for them.

Buffering also frequently occurs in roles that normally require the appearance of authentic concern for the health, welfare or well-being of others. Thus, dentists provide the treatment whilst the receptionist attends to the payments, Father Christmas acts warmly towards children whilst the photographer sells pictures and ministers speak of God's love whilst ushers collect the money offerings.[17] In this way, buffering preserves the image of personal concern that is separate from financial gain.

'Normalizing' emotion

No matter how much we try and control our emotions, it is inevitable that unwanted emotions will still occasionally leak out at work (or outside of work). Luckily, there are ways of minimizing this emotional leakage by using 'normalizing' techniques. This involves diffusing or lessening the impact of the emotion leaked, or somehow changing the way the emotion displayed should be interpreted. One way to do this is simply to apologize for the inappropriate emotional outburst. This usually diffuses the emotion and lessens the reaction immediately. Another technique is to use humour to release an emotion in a more appropriate way. For instance, police officers may use jokes and sarcasm to vent their fear in certain situations – without allowing the real emotion of fear to leak out too clearly.[18]

Another common way of 'normalizing' emotion is to wrap it up in the guise of rationality. Thus, imagine that you are working in a company that is proposing to merge with a larger company. Your immediate reaction might be to say 'no'. In doing this, you have leaked your emotion of fear about the proposed change. To cover this fear up again, what you do is come up with a rational explanation as to why the proposed merger may not work. This is a way of 'normalizing' the fear with rationality.

Surface acting

What emotion management is really all about, of course, is acting. This is reflected in the comment made by one doctor who felt that he was constantly having to manage his emotions as he switched from one script to another. He asked wistfully, 'Are all general practitioners actors basically anyway?'[19] The answer is 'probably', since there are many who argue that as we are engaged in emotion management throughout our lives, we are all 'actors basically anyway':

> *'All of us are amateur actors portraying many different characters in our quest to please the various audiences who sit in social judgement and determine our fate.'*[20]

> *'Certainly it is true that there is a sense in which everybody is acting all the time, playing various roles such as parent and child, professor or student, successful business person or needy poor.'*[21]

> *'Think of life as an unending masquerade party. Compelled to play many roles, we are constantly changing our costumes and masks.'*[22]

We are actors because we care, for whatever reasons, about what other people think of us. Our jobs or livelihoods may depend on making the right impression. Certainly in interviews it is crucial that we act the part and create just the right impression. In day-to-day life, we crave love and friendship and this may involve a little social acting in order to express appropriate emotions and hide inappropriate ones.

People who work in customer service roles may act more than most. Indeed, one airline recognized this explicitly by noting that their employees were 'selected for being able to act well . . . they had to appear at home on stage'.[3] Smiling, appearing pleasant and friendly, being cheerful – all these aspect of the 'Have a Nice Day' culture are likely to involve a degree of acting ability. True, there are some people who are naturally cheerful most of the time, but even these people at times will have to act. There will be times, for instance, when they are feeling unwell, have had bad news or are just worried about something – even in these circumstances they are expected to stick to the script and this means they will have to act. For most of us, however, this acting is part and parcel of everyday life and is not restricted to work life. For instance, the double Academy Award-winning actor Tom Hanks discussed in a recent interview how his acting skills are sharpened by the demands of family life: 'Every parent will tell you that half of keeping discipline in a family is about good acting . . . Think of all the times when you have to put on a really serious face when your kid has gone and done something or other that's really goofy, but you can't let them know that you're amused . . . On the outside you have to keep up your stern face while inside you're actually laughing.'[22]

There are two main ways to succeed at social acting, whether it is so that you can stick to the script required by your job, or so that you can create the right impression in a social situation. Both techniques are based on methods used by professional actors on the stage or in front of the camera. The first technique is called 'surface acting' and this involves simply arranging your physical features so that they reflect the emotion that you want to display. In other words, in surface acting, we don't actually need to feel the emotion we are trying to portray at all. As one researcher put it, 'In surface acting, we deceive others about what we really feel but we do not deceive ourselves.'[3] We can convince others that we feel the appropriate emotion although we are well aware that we are merely acting.

Surface acting is akin to the so-called 'technical' school of professional acting. Actors who follow this approach argue that by not actually feeling the required emotion, they can focus their efforts on the techniques of movement, choreography, positioning and voice control etc in order to portray the emotion needed. If they were to try to actually feel the emotion too, they might get carried away with the feeling and forget crucial elements such as to face the audience, turn to Camera 2 etc that are essential for a successful performance.

Deep acting

'I can psyche myself up – I can trick my brain into believing something that might not be true.'   Supermarket clerk[20]

'The flight attendant is obliged not only to smile, but to try and work up some warmth behind it.'[3]

'Sometimes we try to stir up a feeling we wish we had, and at other times we try to block or weaken a feeling we wish we did not have.'[3]

The difference between surface and deep acting is that in deep acting, the actor attempts to actually try to experience or feel the emotion they wish to display or that is expected and in this way 'deep acting has . . . the edge over simple pretending in its power to convince'.[3] Thus, deep acting, whilst perhaps harder work, is the more effective emotion management technique. Feelings or emotions are actively induced as the actor 'psyches' him or herself into the desired role. It is similar to the way professional actors from the 'method' school of acting psyche themselves up for a part by getting into role and imagining that they are that person. Some method actors engage in months of research to 'become' the person they are playing, even changing their physical appearance to get in the role.

This may be all well and good for professional actors, trained in method acting, but is it really possible for the rest of us to psyche ourselves into the role of concerned counsellor, distressed colleague, excited subordinate or caring shop assistant? The founder of the school of method acting, Stanislavski, advised actors to use 'emotional memory' in order to help them get into role and there is no reason why the rest of us social actors cannot use the same technique. Actors use emotional memory when they are trying to feel a required emotion: it involves the actor trying to 'recall an occasion when a similar circumstance had occurred within his own life and reconstruct the emotion he felt at that time'.[21] Social actors can also use this technique, for instance, thinking of a relative's death when they need to appear sad. Consider the following case studies of examples of how ordinary people can use deep acting techniques to manage their emotions:

Case study 1

Tony works in the customer care department of a large department store. He frequently deals with complaints and his line manager has recently told him that his manner when dealing with complaints needs some working on. 'You just don't seem to care,' she told him. Tony takes up the story:

'The reason that I didn't seem to care was that I really didn't care! The first couple of complaints you do deal with sensitively, but after a while, they just become problems, not people. I don't care if the three-piece suite they had delivered has a mark on it or if their hi-fi system has broken down. They are just problems to be processed. But my boss had made it clear to me that my attitude was wrong and that I would have to appear more caring. So what I do now is, I try and put myself in their shoes. I try and remember a situation that I have been in when I felt as frustrated as them. It's quite hard work – it requires a bit of effort, but it does work.'

Case study 2

Carol is a counsellor who is feeling more than a little burned out. She says:

'I just find it hard to care about my clients any more. Each time a new client comes in I wait to hear their problem and then my heart sinks when I realize that it is that old problem again, or this one. The same issues reoccur with different people. It's so hard to muster up the required empathy over and over again. But empathy is a crucial part of the coun-selling process – without it, it would not be ethical for me to work. So, I try and make myself feel empathy by imagining what it would be like if the person sitting in front of me was my mother, sister, brother etc. How would I feel if the client was someone I really cared about? To help, I try and remember situations when people I have cared about have had problems. Then the empathy and sympathy was genuine, so I just remember those feelings and transfer them onto my patient.'

Case study 3

Martin is a management consultant and also, coincidentally, an ex-actor. He says:

'When I give presentations or pep talks, I like to be really enthusi-astic. But sometimes I don't feel enthusiastic . . . maybe because I have had a hard day, just lost a contract or have personal problems. I use acting skills to make myself feel the enthusiasm again. It is no good, though, just acting enthusiastic – I have to make myself really feel it. I do this by stopping, taking a deep breath and by reminding myself of all the reasons to feel positive and enthusiastic. I remember how I felt when I won a contract or when things were going well. This way I can get myself into gear again.'

This chapter has discussed the various scripts that exist at work and the emotional display rules that are associated with them. A number of techniques to help you adhere to these display rules and manage your emotions even when you are really feeling some contrasting emotion are presented. Of course, emotion management techniques are not always in the full control of the employee. More often than not, it is the company that controls your emotions and they do this by writing your script for you. The next chapter will examine the techniques that companies use to get you to manage your emotions at work.

CHAPTER 4

BECOMING A ONE-MINUTE FRIEND – HOW TO MANAGE YOUR EMOTIONS TO GET THE JOB AND KEEP THE JOB

Although there are at least three different kinds of culture that organizations create in relation to the emotion that their employees are expected to display, the one that is most commonly encouraged, as discussed earlier, is the 'Have a Nice Day' culture. Using display rules and 'fast-food server' scripts, employers go to great lengths to ensure that their staff create just the right cheery and friendly emotional culture for their customers. As I have said before, this is because being nice pays.

Scripts and cultures do not just happen or evolve by themselves. Employers and managers of at least the larger companies (and the ones with the strongest competitive edge) will have thought out and developed a very careful plan aimed at teaching staff the rules and the script from the moment they first approach the company for a job, right up to the point when they are promoted months or years down the line. There are three main stages at which employers are likely to start teaching you the rules of their culture: at the recruitment stage, in the first few weeks of the new job and then throughout the rest of your time in the post. Each stage will be examined separately and tips given on how to succeed at each stage.

AT THE RECRUITMENT STAGE

'We are looking for people with big personalities, so that no matter how tough the going gets, they can smile through until the end.'
Cheerleader recruiter talking on a local radio station in
Manchester, March 1996.

One way that employers can increase the chances that their staff will display exactly the sort of emotions that are in keeping with their corporate image is to recruit only those people who demonstrate that they can express the right emotions. If a company wants friendly staff, it will look for friendly people at the interview stage. A company can even select out those potentially unfriendly people prior to interview, by stating in recruitment advertisements exactly the kind of emotional types being sought. For example, a recruitment advert for *Next* fashion in the UK stated that the people being sought must be 'enthusiastic . . . with a sunny disposition' (ad seen in Manchester store window, June 1998) whilst a recruitment advert for McDonald's spotted on a billboard in Waco, Texas (May 1998) proclaimed: 'We pay for your smiles'. The *Next* advert immediately tells potential applicants that they will be required to be cheerful and if they do not have this quality in their personality, they should not apply. The McDonald's ad similarly tells potential recruits straight away that the main requirement of the job is to smile; *that* is what they will be paid for, rather than any specific ability to serve or cook. The subtext of both these adverts is that anyone who feels unable to smile all the time or who does not want to, need not apply.

Once an applicant has been shortlisted, there are a number of techniques that employers can use to select only those people who feel (or rather *appear* to feel) the 'right' emotions:

Interview

Most companies use the interview situation in order to select applicants. Many candidates think that the interviewers are looking for specific characteristics, skills, experiences and abilities, and, whilst this may be true, they are also undoubtedly looking for the appropriate emotional display too. Research has shown that job prospects are much better for interviewees who convey positive emotions and who hide negative feelings. For instance, one study showed that interviewees who smiled and maintained eye contact with their interviewers were more likely to be offered jobs than people whose faces showed a 'more neutral facial expression and less smiling'.[1]

So, what kind of emotions are recruiters looking for? The most common ones amongst the 'Have a Nice Day' cultures are enthusiasm and friendliness, as illustrated by a number of real-life examples:

• A manual produced by McDonald's 'Hamburger University' (where new recruits learn the skills of producing and serving the perfect standardized smile as well as the perfect standardized hamburger) states that servers must 'display desirable traits such as sincerity, enthusiasm, confidence and a sense of humor'.[2]

- Continental Airlines seek people who 'convey a sprit of enthusiasm'.[3]

- Delta Airlines look for people who are 'enthusiastic with calm and poise'.[3]

- In Greece, the Greek hotel chain Grecotel 'looks for signs of friendliness' at the initial interview.[4]

Case study

I once asked a recruitment manager for a large postal company exactly what he was looking for in the people he was interviewing. His answer was simple:

'I am looking for the person who bangs his or her fist on the table and shouts "I want this job!", in other words, I want them to be enthusiastic and excited. If they can really demonstrate a strong desire to do the job, then I think they will stick at it and succeed.'

On the other hand, companies that operate in 'Have a Cool Day' or even 'Have a Rotten Day' cultures are obviously looking for different kinds of emotional displays. For example, a debt-collecting agency studied in 1991 looked for people who could display 'a bit or irritation'[5] and they did this by looking for aggressiveness in potential recruits.

Top Tip: Always find out what the emotional culture is of the organization you are hoping to work for. You can do this by visiting other branches (if the company is a chain) and noticing whether the staff smile or are sullen. Other ways of sussing out the culture include visiting their Website (most companies have one) and looking for clues such as words like 'warm', 'friendly', 'cheerful', or looking them up in newspapers to see what stories, if any, have been printed about them. Then, display the emotions conducive to that culture at the interview.

Observation of product interaction

When the business of the company involves a particular product, or set of products, the employer is likely to search for people who appear to display the right emotions about that product. Most employers want the job applicants to be as excited and enthusiastic about the product as they themselves are. This is especially true if the recruiter is the one who was actually involved in the design or the commissioning of the product. For instance, members of the team that designed Apple's Macintosh computer sought new employees who shared their wild enthusiasm for the computer. A key part of the selection process involved showing the new machines to the applicants and watching to see if they reacted with 'exaggerated enthusiasm'.[6]

Case study

'I attended an interview once with two other candidates. We were shown round the department and the computing facilities. Two of us made all the right noises about the facilities – marvelling about the state-of-the-art equipment and the quantity available, but the third candidate was very critical. He claimed that their highest spec computer would not be powerful enough for the work the job involved and that he was surprised by their choice of a now-obsolete printer. He also criticized the quality of the output, saying that he could get better quality on his home computer. We were shocked – as was the person showing us round. It was obvious he wouldn't get the job.'

Top Tip: If you go for an interview or selection process for a company and are shown the product that you will be required to sell or work with, pretend to be enthralled and excited, even if you are not! This applies to any physical aspect of the work environment that you are shown. If the new reception area is proudly displayed, react appropriately.

'Animation' tests

Animation tests are designed to test interpersonal skills. The idea is that people who can be friendly, cheerful and upbeat will appear animated and this can be tested by having applicants interact with each other informally. For instance, Pan American Airlines used this technique to select those people who could display the necessary good cheer that the job role would require.[3] Another example is given in the following case study:

Case study

A Youth Agency was seeking to recruit a new youth worker and part of the person specification (ie the characteristics being sought) included having a friendly, upbeat and cheerful personality. They tested this by having applicants interact with a group of youths in order to ascertain how 'animated' the applicants were when working with young people.

They found that one applicant who had appeared very enthusiastic in the interview was unable to build a warm rapport with the young people and so was de-selected.

Many companies use animation tests in a rather more sneaky way than this. For instance, they will invite the candidates to have a chat over lunch, or to have look around the building the day before the interview. Any situation that involves contact with other people may well be assessed as an animation test.

Top Tip: Be animated at all times! This means at lunch, over coffee, when being shown around, when interacting with the secretary, or even with the tealady. You never know when you are being subjected to an animation test.

Mock work tests

This technique involves giving the applicant a task to do that is actually part of the real job (or would be if the applicant was successful) and seeing what kind of emotions they display whilst carrying out the task. For instance, applicants may be asked to interact with customers, to deliver mail, serve food or whatever it is that may be required in the job. This can be quite a difficult test since the applicant may be concentrating more on the technical aspects of completing the task than on the emotional aspects of display.

Case study

A public relations company in the UK was recruiting staff and had short-listed to the final three. One of the characteristics that they were seeking was the ability to be 'tough' with clients. In other words, they did not necessarily want staff to be part of a 'Have a Nice Day' culture, since sometimes they would have to follow 'lawyer'-type script. For instance, clients could be very insensitive and abrupt, especially in times of stress, and the ideal candidate would have to be able to stay calm and emotionless even when they were not being treated with respect and courtesy.

Their mock test involved a rather bizarre exercise of swearing and shouting at the prospective employee. Those that stood their ground and remained calm and neutral succeeded in the test. Those that reacted with any kind of emotion such as anger were not considered suitable.

Top Tip: Remember that you might be given a mock work test without even knowing! Some people are subjected to the most soul-destroying interviews, only to discover that how they reacted was what was actually being judged. Always find out what the emotional culture of the organization you are applying to is, then display the appropriate emotions, no matter what (but within reason – this does not mean that you should allow yourself to be verbally abused or insulted in an interview situation).

Trial periods

Companies which require emotional control over long periods of time (as opposed to just short bursts) may well employ a trial period. This actually makes very good sense for the employer since many people are capable of acting for a short period of time; maintaining the act over extensive time periods is much harder (and probably more stressful, as will be discussed in chapter 7). The companies that use trial periods in this way are likely to be in the service industry. One industry that commonly uses this practice is the airline industry, where flight attendants have to maintain the displayed emotion for a long time (especially on long-haul flights) and often in the face of abuse or pressure. For instance, Delta Airlines are reported to use a trial period to determine if new staff have what they call the 'emotional stamina' to 'exude good cheer during long, crowded flights'[5] and to maintain a 'steady level of enthusiasm despite the long hours and arduous schedule'.[3] Trial periods are much better indicators of ability to display the appropriate emotions than interviews.

Top Tip: Acting over long periods can be stressful (see chapter 7), so if, during a trial period, you find that your smile is continually faked, it may be worth considering a different kind of job. It is important that your personality fits the environment in which you are working, and if you are constantly faking, then you are likely to be stressed by this lack of 'person–environment fit'. On the other hand, expect some faking as part and parcel of the job.

DURING THE FIRST FEW WEEKS IN THE NEW JOB

Once the new recruit has successfully passed the recruitment phase and has managed to convince the employer that he or she can express the right emotions, you might think that the employer would be satisfied.

After all, they have already gone to considerable lengths to ensure that the people who now work for them (and who may well represent the company to the public) are capable of displaying – and likely to display – the desired emotions. But, in fact, the efforts that the employer goes to in order to control the emotional display of its employees has only just begun. The strategy continues in earnest once the new recruit takes up his or her post.

The main technique used by companies in the early stage of a new recruit's work life is what is called *socialization*. This is a method that refers to new recruits learning the rules by observing the behaviour of other people, by learning the rulebooks or by attending training programmes. They become *socialized* into the new emotional culture. For example:

- In the personnel manual given to new recruits of the Greek hotel chain, Grecotel, it is explained under a section entitled 'smiling' that 'it is very important that our greeting is followed by a warm smile'.[4]

- The ice-cream chain Häagen-Dazs issues its serving staff with special order pads with instructions printed on each sheet to prime the server to smile when serving customers (order sheet taken, with permission, from Manchester restaurant, September 1997).

- Walt Disney World use classes, handbooks and billboards to teach newcomers that they must convey emotions that make customers feel good about themselves (emotions consistent with the 'Have a Nice Day' culture). Newcomers learn the distinction between being 'on-stage' (where Disney patrons or 'guests' can go) and being 'off-stage' (where only employees are allowed). When on-stage employees (or 'performers') must follow precise guidelines about which emotions can and cannot be expressed in order to 'create happiness' (BBC1 television programme, *Holiday: Fasten your seatbelt*, 29 April 1997). Newcomers are told 'you were cast for role, not hired for job' and 'our audience is composed of guests, not customers'.[7,8,9] The use of such metaphors allows the new recruit to be socialized into the emotional culture that encourages the display of good cheer, friendliness and warmth.

- Safeway supermarket clerks are told in training manuals to be 'friendly with the customers' and even to 'read the customer's name off the check and use the name when thanking the customer'.[10]

- On the opposite end of the spectrum, debt collectors are taught to convey negative feeling and the social means of maintaining this are illustrated by one trainer who admonished, 'Come on, don't be such a wimp. You've got to be more intense – where is the urgency in your voice?'[5]

Many organizations do not have such a formal socialization process to control employees' emotions. That is, they are not always written into handbooks or manuals. Very often, the emotional culture is taught to new recruits through a process of social learning whereby newcomers learn the rules about emotional expression by watching and observing others and then by copying or imitating the emotions displayed. For instance, by observing experienced surgeons medical students learn that mild compassion is the expected emotional demeanour and that it may even be acceptable to treat patients with indifference.[11]

During the first few weeks in the new job, newcomers learn about not only those emotional expressions they should display to customers or clients, but also to each other – to co-workers and colleagues. Thus, for example, medical students who express too much sadness on the death of a patient are likely to be told by more experienced colleagues not to get too emotionally involved.

The following case studies illustrate how powerfully the socialization process can work for new recruits:

Case study 1
Jeff started a new job as a car salesman and tells of the different emotional displays that he learned to express by copying his colleagues:

'I assumed when I started work that I would have to be nice and smiley, if not downright ingratiating, to all customers. But I watched my colleagues, and noticed that they behaved differently to different types of customers. For instance, they can spot the time-wasters and are much cooler towards them. You can often tell the time-wasters – they are usually young men who are dressed scruffily. Our cars are top of the range. I once got teased mercilessly for spending one and a half hours trying to sell a car to a time-waster. Now I am cooler towards them.'

Case study 2
Julie is a nurse who began work in Intensive Care after working for many years on a surgical ward. She says:

'The emotional culture was very different in Intensive Care, but no one actually told me the rules. I had to pick them up as I went along. For instance, we are allowed to express more sympathy to patients' families and spend time comforting them. We don't have to present such a distance as on other wards. We also have to switch very quickly from one demeanour to another – for example, I could be having a laugh with a colleague, but as soon as I walk onto the ward, I am expected to arrange my face into a totally different expression.'

Top Tip: In the first few weeks of a new job, you should look around you and observe how your more experienced colleagues display their emotions. Is it a 'Have a Nice Day' culture, a 'Have a Cool Day' one or a 'Have a Rotten Day' culture? Do the scripts switch – are your colleagues nice and friendly to customers/clients but not to the boss? Or are they honest with their emotions with each other (be careful to suss out if they are *really* honest as there is often a great deal of emotion management between colleagues too) but not with the boss? Before letting off steam with anyone, always suss out the emotional culture first. The table overleaf should help.

THROUGHOUT THE FOLLOWING MONTHS AND YEARS

The attempts at emotion management do not stop after the first few weeks of induction for the new recruit. Emotion management by the employer is an on-going activity that often lasts the lifetime of the worker. The employee's attempts at conforming to the required emotional culture are often checked and may be implicitly or explicitly rewarded (or punished) in order to encourage the appropriate displays to be expressed. Punishments for not displaying the right emotions can be severe. For example, the researcher who studied the 'Have a Rotten Day' culture of the debt collector noted that 'even experienced collectors occasionally were fired because they could not control their tempers'.[5] Such debt collectors had very specific scripts and, whilst they were expected to display anger and irritation, they were not expected to actually lose their tempers (and, by implication, control of themselves and the situation). In other words, they were expected to act, rather than really get emotionally involved.

Other less severe means of punishing workers who stray from the script are widely used and these usually involve some kind of financial reward – or withholding of such reward. These can include promotion,

Type of culture	Main identifiable features
The total 'Have a Nice Day' culture	• Staff are expected to be warm and friendly to each other. • Customers are to be smiled at, thanked politely and wished a pleasant day. • Negative emotions such as anger or boredom are suppressed. • Displays of enthusiasm and interest are desired at all times.
The frontline 'Have a Nice Day' culture	• Staff are only expected to be 'nice' to customers. • Employees are expected to be honest with each other and with their superiors. • Staff are allowed to let off steam after dealing with abusive customers. • Negative emotions are allowed amongst colleagues.
The 'Have a Cool Day' culture	• Staff are not expected to display any emotions. • Employees appear aloof and distant. • Real feelings are hidden behind a neutral front.
The 'Have a Rotten Day' culture	• Only negative feelings are expressed. • Positive happy emotions are suppressed. • The aim is to make others feel intimidated or threatened.

cash prizes, gifts, pay rises and, perhaps the most underestimated of all rewards, praise. Many workers can be encouraged to repeat appropriate and desired behaviour by rewarding them with praise. On the other hand, punishments can include criticism, warnings, and demotions as well as firings. In the case of the bill collectors mentioned above, these rewards and punishments were administered by supervisors who monitored the phone conversations that collectors had with the debtors from whom they were trying to obtain owed monies. One supervisor was heard to criticize a collector for not expressing the appropriate emotions – 'she isn't conveying any urgency at all. She won't get a dime'.[3] Another example of rewarding appropriate emotion is shown by a supermarket whose clerks were rewarded with twenty-five-dollar bonuses if caught displaying the 'required cheer' by check-ers whilst those in another supermarket who were observed 'greeting, smiling, establishing eye contact and saying "thank you"' could even win a new car.[12]

Case study

'I work in a hotel that has an "employee of the month" scheme. The winner wears a special pin on their lapel and has privileges such as a reserved car parking space for the month. To win, you need to be really nice to customers! They have to nominate you, but you also have to be seen to be nice, overly helpful and friendly by the boss. Obviously, we tend to be nicer when the boss is around, since being nice to customers alone wasn't enough – this was because many customers are very complacent about filling in those forms. The addition of the boss as a judge was meant to make it fairer, but it just meant that we put more energy into being nice when the boss was within earshot.'

Rewards and punishments for displaying the right emotions can even be meted out by the customer (as in the case study above) who is co-opted by management to assess the emotional displays of the worker. Many supermarkets, for instance (especially in North America), have a 'customer's bill of rights' prominently displayed and they encourage customers to inform management of any violation of these rights. In a 1989 Safeway television advertisement, the head office of the chain invited customers who were unhappy with the service in any Safeway store to call a freephone number. At Albertson's (an Idaho-based chain), clerks who failed to provide adequate customer service were required to present the complaining customer with a gift of a dozen eggs. At Winn-Dixie stores (a Southern US chain) during a 'courtesy campaign', clerks wore dollar bills pinned to their clothes; if a checker failed to provide the customer with a friendly greeting and sincere 'thank you' the customer received a dollar (all examples taken from Tolich[10]).

Another common example of the customer being co-opted by man-agement to judge emotional displays is in the now-frequent messages on the back of trucks and other company vehicles that ask, 'Am I driving courteously? If not call 1–800 (or 0800) . . .'. This shows how emotional display can even be considered important on the road when driving a truck. The following case study illustrates the point:

Case study

Deborah was infuriated one day by the rudeness shown by a driver of a courier company truck. She says:

'The guy was so rude – first he cut in front of me, then he hogged the whole lane and did not show any concern or courtesy for anyone else. I was so mad that I actually called the number on the back of his truck. I rang the company and told them what happened. They were very apologetic and said they would look into it. I didn't expect to hear any more, but they rang me the next day and said that they had investigated my complaint and the driver in question had been fined.'

Top Tip: The tip here then is to always be on your guard. Many companies, especially those in the service industry, have the 'mystery shopper' concept whereby a staff member pretends to be a customer in order to establish what kind of service is on offer (if service companies do not have mystery shoppers, they really ought to). Always display the appropriate emotions, even if sometimes you have to act.

This chapter has shown how organizations use various methods to control the emotional displays of their employees from day one (and even before day one). The implications of this are that workers should strive to meet the emotional requirements or display rules of the company in order to get and keep the job. The problem with doing this is that the worker may start to experience 'emotional labour', a concept that is introduced in the next chapter.

CHAPTER 5

'EMOTIONAL LABOUR' – THE MENTAL EFFORT INVOLVED IN MANAGING YOUR EMOTIONS

So far, I have discussed emotional control at work in terms of the strategies that employers and employees can use in order to manage or control the emotional displays that they present at work. This emotion management is an important part of work life, since it is inevitable that few of us are able to genuinely display the emotions that are required by our employer at all times. At least sometimes, we will have to fake our displays, whilst simultaneously hiding how we really feel. This requires a great deal of mental energy and effort as we work on or *labour* on our emotional displays. For this reason, the effort involved in managing or controlling our emotions at work is termed 'emotional labour'. As one source puts it, 'to comply with emotional codes . . . people will privately labour with, or do work on, their feelings, in order to create the socially desired expression'.[1]

The following contemporary examples illustrate this concept of emotional labour in the working lives of ordinary people such as secretaries, waiters, receptionists, hairdressers, bill collectors, funeral directors, salespeople, flight attendants and even beauty consultants:

'The secretary who creates a cheerful office that announces her company as "friendly and dependable" . . . , the waitress or waiter who creates an "atmosphere of pleasant dining", the tour guide or hotel receptionist who makes us feel welcome, the social worker whose look of solicitous concern makes the client feel cared for, the salesman who creates the sense of a "hot commodity", the bill collector who inspires fear, the funeral director who makes the bereaved feel understood . . . all of them must confront in some way or another the requirements of emotional labour.'[2]

'In telephone sales you've got to be nice no matter what, and lots of times I don't feel like being nice. To act enthusiastic is hard work for me.'   Bill Collector.[2]

'Waiters in fancy restaurants routinely convey the required polite demeanour while simultaneously feeling angry towards rude patrons.'[3]

'Mary Kay teaches her beauty consultants to offer fake enthusiasm to customers when they don't feel genuine enthusiasm.'[4]

'If you don't like people, you can't tell them that, can you? You've got to be nice to them, instead of telling them what you really feel like, like kicking them . . . you've got to be nice to them. If you don't like them, you've got to put a brave face on.'
                                                             Trainee Hairdresser[5]

'For the flight attendant, the smiles are a part of her work . . . Similarly, part of the job is to disguise fatigue and irritation, for otherwise . . . the product – passenger contentment – would be damaged.'[2]

'Organizations continue to manage hearts by calling on employees to exhibit forced niceness, phony smiles and suppressed anger.'[6]

Each of these examples illustrates the faking of unfelt emotion and/or the suppressing of felt emotion – because of the demands of the work role. Thus, emotional labour has three potential components:

- It involves the faking of emotion that is not really felt,

- and/or the hiding of emotion that *is* felt.

- This emotion management is performed in order to meet social expectation – usually as part of the job role.

In order for emotion management to be classified as 'emotional labour', at least one of the first two components must exist, in addition to the third. If one of these necessary components is absent, then emotional labour is not being performed.

The emotions that we express at work (or in any social setting) do not always result in the performing of emotional labour, of course. Our emotional displays can match well or poorly with both our true feelings and with display rules (see chapter 2). If our emotional display matches the display rules or social expectation AND reflects how we really feel, then we are said to be in a state of *emotional harmony*. No emotional labour is experienced. If, on the other hand, the emotions that we display match the display rules of the organization but are different from those that we really feel, we are said to be in a state of *emotional dissonance* and emotional labour is experienced. A third state exists when our emotional display matches how we really feel but is different from that which we are expected to display (ie display rules) – this is termed *emotional deviance* and does not involve emotional labour. Each of these states is shown in the following table and will be discussed in more detail in the sections that follow.

An illustration of emotional harmony, dissonance and deviance (based on work by Briner[7])

	Emotional harmony	Emotional dissonance	Emotional deviance
	(displayed emotion is the same as felt emotion and expected emotion)	(displayed emotion is the same as expected emotion but different from felt emotion)	(displayed emotion is the same as felt emotion but different from expected emotion)
Emotion actually displayed	☺	☺	☺
Emotion really felt	☺	☹	☺
Emotion expected by company society (display rule)	☺	☺	☹

As mentioned, emotional labour occurs mainly when we are in a state of emotional dissonance – when our real feelings are different from those expected and displayed. There are many examples of emotional labourers and some were described at the beginning of this chapter. But consider too the cocktail waitress who must appear 'exuberant and friendly' even to abusive customers if tips are to be forthcoming,[8] or the doctor who must suppress her feelings in front of patients, only to 'cry and weep when patients left her surgery'.[9] Consider also the foreman on the shopfloor who must enforce work rules that he thinks are 'inane',[10] or the police officer who is required to be 'calm and dispassionate in the face of human misery'[11] or the worker who told one researcher that 'even when people are paid to be nice, it's hard to be nice at all times'.[2] In each of these real-life examples, managing emotions and performing emotional labour is a crucial element to success at the job. More examples will be given in later sections.

EMOTIONAL HARMONY

'The wonderful thing is that those people make us mad and we are supposed to let them know that we are mad at them!'

Debt Collector[12]

Emotional harmony is probably the most comfortable and least stressful state to be in. The emotions we are expressing are precisely those emotions that we genuinely feel and coincide exactly with those emotions that we are expected to display. Shop assistants who really feel happy and cheerful can perform in a 'Have a Nice Day' culture with a genuine manner. They are expected to feel cheerful, they do indeed feel cheerful and the expression on their face is cheerful. Traffic wardens or car clampers who are feeling angry and miserable can be curt and abrupt (in a 'Have a Rotten Day' culture) to parking violators in an entirely genuine manner. In this case, they are expected to be angry and surly, they do indeed feel this way and the expression on their faces is also surly. In both cases, the workers are existing in a comfortable state of emotional harmony. The following case studies offer some real-life examples:

Case study 1
'I work in a flower shop and most of my customers come into the shop in good moods. They are really cheery and happy – they are usually buying flowers because they are in love, are celebrating a birthday, are thanking someone for something – all good things that make them happy. Because of this, I love my job! I am a fairly happy sort of person,

and I love sharing in other people's joy. I always ask questions like, "when was the baby born?", "when is the wedding?" etc so I can share the happy occasion more. Of course, some customers come in to buy funeral arrangements, so it's not all joy!'

Case study 2

'My job involves my being nice and friendly to people all the time – I greet people as they walk into a store. When I feel happy and cheerful, I love my job. What could be better than spending all day being allowed to be happy and cheery? Sometimes, I am really cheery and just want to tip my hat and chirp "top of the morning to you!" – which is exactly what I am meant to do! On the other hand, if I feel down in the dumps, it is really hard work to put on the happy act.'

People who continually work in jobs that allow them to be in states of emotional harmony are probably in the job that really suits their personality. However, it is rare to find people who always work in emotional harmony since it is almost inevitable that there will be times when our displayed emotion will not match our true feelings. It is at these times that we experience emotional dissonance.

EMOTIONAL DISSONANCE

> 'We have to sing the praises of God sometimes when we are not feeling very much like praising God. Or we have to mourn and lament when we are feeling extremely happy.'
>
> Nun talking about her job on the BBC1 TV
> programme *Everyman*, 4 February 1996

Emotional dissonance occurs when the emotions we express satisfy social expectation or display rules, but clash with how we really feel. This is emotional labour which has been described as an 'integral yet often unrecognized part of employment that involves contact with people'.[13] Emotional labour is a relatively new concept in that it has only started to be given attention in recent years. It very often involves a great deal of acting skill – something that is not lost on many employees, as demonstrated by the Cathay Pacific flight attendant who commented that 'we say we are all entertainers now because everyone is on stage'.[14] The following real-life case studies illustrate the existence of emotional labour:

Case study 1

'I was celebrating a birthday at a well-known American bistro where the staff all come over and sing a birthday tune. There were five staff members and I noticed one very miserable-looking woman at the end. She looked so surly and angry, yet she had to clap and sing this cheery song! Whilst the other staff smiled and laughed, she managed the entire song without smiling but looking gloomy. The only time she smiled was at the end – and that smile was directed to her colleagues, not me.'

Case study 2

'The hardest thing is being polite to someone who is being completely illogical in directing their anger at you. You have to stay polite – even when they are taking their anger out on you inappropriately. It's my job to be polite on behalf of the people I work for. That is really bottling up your emotions! I also find it hard with subordinates – if they do something wrong I want to scream at them, but have to try and be calm and patient.'

Performing emotional labour can have a lot of benefits for both the labourer or actor and for the organization (to say nothing of the customer) and these will be discussed later in this chapter. However, there are also a number of potential costs to emotional labour performance, and these will be outlined in detail in the next chapter. Before discussing the benefits of emotional labour performance, let us examine that rare third state that can exist – emotional deviance.

EMOTIONAL DEVIANCE

This state occurs when we display the emotions that we really feel but that clash with display rules or expectation. Every time we walk into a store and the assistant is rude or scowling, we can be sure (at least in many countries) that they are operating under emotional deviance. Psychologically, this is not an unhealthy state, since real feelings are being expressed (see next chapter). However, it is not a healthy state in terms of financial reward, since workers in states of emotional deviance are not as likely to get promoted, receive tips or praise etc. In fact, if their emotional deviance is spotted, they are likely to be punished or even fired (see last chapter). The following case studies demonstrate the factors that can lead to emotional deviance:

Case study 1

'When you are dealing with customer after customer, you stop caring. I work in a complaints department answering the phone and the line rings incessantly. By the end of the day, I don't care about the customers at all, and I am often shorter or more curt that I should be. I know that I should be polite and courteous, but, frankly, it's just too much effort.'

Case study 2

'Part of my training as a store assistant involves being told to be nice and smiley to everyone. But, I only do this when I know I am being watched by the boss! If she is within sight, I am as nice as pie. The rest of the time I look bored because I am bored. I mean, we spend half our time folding and unfolding sweaters! It's such an effort not to look bored that I save it for when it matters.'

Emotional deviance may be a way of dealing with the stress of emotional labour that will be discussed at length in the next chapter, but is not a coping mechanism that is recommended! (For coping mechanisms that *are* recommenced, see chapter 8.) There is a very good chance that people working in states of deviance will be 'caught out' – usually by a customer complaining to the boss or manager about the surly waiter, miserable bank clerk or unfriendly receptionist. Operating under emotional deviance may seem the easy option, but it will not benefit you in the long term. Besides, emotional labour may be hard mental work, but it does have a number of benefits, as the next section demonstrates.

BENEFITS OF EMOTIONAL LABOUR PERFORMANCE

Emotional labour performance has a great many benefits for the labourer, for the organization and for the customer/client or colleagues of the labourer. The following real-life examples go some way to illustrating the benefits that emotional labour performance can have:

> 'Loyal, regular customers are a source of steady sales for your store. Smile! Service with a smile and a friendly attitude will keep them loyal and keep them coming back!'
>
> From a training programme used by a
> chain of convenience stores in the USA[15]

'In the checkstand, it takes a smile, a friendly attitude, courteous service . . . and good appearance to make a customer want to come back to Raley's. You may be the last contact with customers as they leave the store. Make it pleasant and memorable.'
From training manual for Raley's store[16]

'A cheerful "Good Morning" and "Good Evening" followed by courteous, attentive treatment and a sincere "Thank you, please come again" will send them away with a friendly feeling and a desire to return.' Supermarket training handbook[15]

'Emotional labour is potentially good. No customer wants to deal with a surly waitress, a crabby bank clerk or a flight attendant who avoids eye contact.'[2]

All these examples show how displaying emotions in accordance with the 'Have a Nice Day' culture is thought to benefit the organization, especially in the service industry. Smiling at customers, say the authors of a recent book, 'often elicits a smile in return, and the creation of a friendly interaction'.[17] In other words, by smiling at customers, *even if we don't feel like smiling* (and thus, when we must perform emotional labour in order to smile), we create a pleasant and friendly environment that makes the customer feel good, makes them want to smile back at us and encourages them to return to the store.

Studies have indeed proved that being nice pays; one training course that urged salespeople to use 'fast-food server' type displays such as a 'friendly, smiling, enthusiastic face' claimed this led to a sales increase of 41 per cent.[18] Another American company, The Southland Corporation, spent over $11 million on a campaign to encourage its supermarket clerks to offer 'good cheer' to customers; they expected increased sales of 2 per cent which would bring in an additional $100 million.[4] These sales increases are expected not only because being nice to customers makes them feel better about themselves and thus more likely to spend money, but also because that happy customer is more likely to return to that store on another occasion – the store thus benefits from so-called 'encore gains' or repeat business; as one source puts it, 'friendly clerks encourage customers to spend more during each visit and to return more frequently'.[4]

But why should this be? Why, exactly, is it that customers will return to a friendly store, even if the products cost a little more or are of slightly inferior quality? The reasons are psychological and form the basis of the field of study called consumer psychology. Evidence from laboratory studies shows that positive feelings about an event make it more accessible to memory and thus more likely to come to mind.[19] Thus, if an event, place or person makes us feel happy or good about ourselves, we are more likely to think about that place or person in the future. This has been related to consumer choice such that researchers have shown that customers who feel good about a particular store are more likely to remember that store the next time they consider where to shop[20] – and customers feel good when employees are nice to them. Many companies recognize this and Continental Airlines do so explicitly when they say in their in-flight video presentation, 'we know that the feeling you take away with you after your flight will influence your choice to use Continental Airlines in the future' (shown on a transatlantic flight, January 1997).

This process whereby being nice to customers encourages them to return could even be the start of a *conditioning response*. Conditioning happens when we are rewarded for doing something – because we are rewarded, we are more likely to repeat the behaviour in future. We become conditioned to performing that behaviour. This is how toddlers are toilet-trained (the reward is praise or other incentives) and how much of human learning occurs. Conversely, conditioning can train us by punishing us for performing undesirable behaviours. We then avoid performing those behaviours in order to avoid the punishment. Thus a child who is slapped for running into the road will avoid repeating this potentially dangerous act (we hope) in order to avoid being punished by his or her parent.

Stores and shops can use this conditioning response that is so much a feature of human learning to condition us to spend our money with them. By their being nice to us and making us feel good, we are rewarded for shopping there and thus become conditioned to repeat the behaviour (shopping at that store) in order to get our reward (feeling good). (Of course now, there are other, more blatant ways that supermarkets encourage a conditioned response. Use of loyalty and reward cards demonstrates to the customer the connection between behaviour and reward much more explicitly.)

Conditioning by punishment can sometimes be used by companies such as debt-collecting agencies who operate in a 'Have a Rotten Day' culture. By displaying unpleasant emotions to debtors, it is hoped that they will pay up in order to avoid the punishment of another phone call or abusive demand for money. We don't even have to be the targets of the punishment ourselves to become conditioned. Just hearing about someone else's experience can make us avoid a particular course of action. For instance, if we hear of a friend who received a speeding ticket on a particular stretch of road, we are likely to reduce our speed when driving on that road. Similarly, hearing about someone's good experience with a store can encourage us to visit that store. This is why a company's image and reputation are its most valuable assets. It is said (see F Lager, *Ben and Jerry's: The Inside Scoop*, Crown Trade Paperbacks, New York, 1995) that if a customer has a complaint with a store that is not solved adequately, he or she will tell ten people. Each of those ten people learns to avoid the problem company. Moreover, each of those ten may tell another ten, who all become conditioned to avoid the offending company. One episode of poor customer service can end up costing the company a great deal not only in terms of reduced repeat business from the dissatisfied customer, but from everyone who gets to hear about the company's failings. On the other hand, if a customer is particularly happy about a company and tells ten people, that is a potentially lucrative customer base that is now open to the company. Thus, being exceptionally nice to customers, even if it involves acting or the performing of emotional labour, is a very wise way to gain a competitive edge over other companies.

The important role of emotional labour performance in building and maintaining a company's image and reputation is reflected in a comment made by an Australian CEO who, when asked how many people were in the public relations department of his firm, replied 'sixteen thousand', which was the total number of employees in the organization.[21] The CEO realized that each employee has the chance to make or break the reputation of the company by the degree to which they were 'believing (or pretending to believe) and acting (or pretending to act) in accordance with the public image they wish to foster'.[22] If just one employee is rude or curt with a customer, *generalization* effects mean that the customer will generalize that rudeness to the entire company. That is, the customer is more likely to think 'Company X is an unfriendly place', rather than 'one of Company X's employees is unfriendly'. By having all employees perform emotional labour, managers can ensure that no customer should ever encounter a discourteous or less than pleasant employee.

Performing emotional labour does not only help the organization – it can also be of great benefit to the worker too. Complying with display rules helps the employee in a number of ways. Firstly, on a basic level, by providing the employee with a script (sometimes literally, other times the 'script' is more of a guide) they have a prescribed set of responses and patterns of behaviour to guide them through almost every eventuality. Consider these case studies that illustrate this point:

Case study 1

'Although I feel constantly irritated about being told when and how often to smile, what to say to customers, etc, sometimes, it can be a relief. I serve in a fast-food restaurant and the work is so boring that I can switch off and let the script take over. I don't have to think about what to say or how to behave – it's all there for me. I just follow it like an actor learns his lines. It's no effort, which means that my mind can be occupied with much more important things like what I need to buy for dinner tonight or what I'll wear on Saturday night.'

Case study 2

'I often get hassle from customers who I wait on in the restaurant. They think that they own me or can say what they like to me. Some call me "girl", others even try and touch me up. Sometimes they just ignore me when I bring them their food. Luckily, I have a response ready for almost every occasion – for instance, if they call me "girl", I look around and then ask them innocently, "Do you mean me?" I don't get tongue-tied or caught on the hop, or spend time later wishing I'd thought of a witty response. We were all given the appropriate words to deal with each situation when we started in the job. We just have to recite them when needed.'

This extra crutch in terms of a script can help give the worker confidence too. It might be that they are faking their emotional display, and that they really want to tell offensive customers how they really feel, but having a script up their sleeves can be a boost to staff who might otherwise be worn down by the treatment by customers. Scripts also make interactions more predictable and avoid embarrassing problems that might occur if we did not perform emotional labour. Consider the following examples of situations where we might fake emotional display in order to avoid feeling awkward or embarrassed:

- If someone tells us a weak joke, we may laugh (even though we do not feel like it) to prevent them feeling awkward.

- If someone trips in the street, we may smile sympathetically (even though we feel like laughing) to reduce their embarrassment.

- If we did not hear or catch a joke properly, or did not understand it, we may laugh to avoid being embarrassed ourselves.

- We may even laugh at jokes we really find offensive in order that we should not be considered aloof.

In all these cases, emotional labour is performed in order to protect ourselves from displaying our true (and inappropriate) emotions. When we put on an act like at work, we may also gain financially from our emotional labour efforts. This could be from a sales commission or in garnering larger tips. For instance, one researcher cites the example of a waitress who reacted so pleasantly to a customer spilling a drink that the customer felt obliged to leave a healthy tip – in fact, the waitress had manipulated the situation so that she spilt the drink but made it look like it was the customer's fault![3] For a salesperson the financial reward may be less directly associated with emotional labour performance – but it is there. The worker who laughs and smiles with customers or clients may perform emotional labour in order to ensure the smooth running of a pleasant interaction. The chances of the other person in the interaction liking them (and thus rewarding them with their business), is greatly increased by their emotional labouring efforts since they are far more likely to create a good impression by smiling at their weak jokes than by scowling. Thus, 'keeping the irritability manageable to get what you want may feel unnatural at first, but it pays dividends in the end'.[23] The following case study from a cosmetics salesman illustrates this point:

Case study
'I sell products from a cosmetics company to companies such as pharmacies and department stores. When I deal with a buyer, I often have to play the game with them before they'll buy. It's not just my sales pitch that counts, but how I treat them is also a factor. I have to really schmooze them – you know, be nice, complimentary, laugh at their jokes, ask about their families, flatter them etc. I build a relationship with them and make them feel good. In return, they try and give my products a better position on the display, or agree to a larger space for the display.'

This is not to suggest that we always perform emotional labour in a Machiavellian manner, with the exclusive goal of ingratiating ourselves in order to gain financially. We may perform emotional labour solely as a 'good-natured endeavour to lubricate the creaking mechanism of social intercourse'.[24] That is, we don't always gain anything other than a more pleasant interaction which makes our world a nicer place. In addition, by faking our emotions we do not necessarily do a disservice to the target of our emotional labour – that is, we are not necessarily tricking them or lying to them. If we go to such efforts to manage our emotions for them, it could be argued that we care enough about them to want them to feel good. This is contrary to the position that some may hold in which it is considered false or hypocritical to fake emotional display. This will be returned to in chapter 7.

Another benefit to performing emotional labour is particularly relevant for those people whose jobs are especially emotionally demanding. Within this category are likely to be:

- nurses

- doctors

- teachers

- funeral attendants

- social workers

- probation officers

- police detectives

These are people for whom work is likely to involve close encounters with misery, struggle and heart-rending if not tragic stories. If they were to genuinely feel the emotions that they have to display all the time, they would spend their working (and, quite possibly, total) lives in abject misery, worry, shock and grief. In order to protect themselves, they can distance themselves emotionally and perform emotional labour instead of actually feeling the emotions. In other words, they act instead of feel. It is for this reason that advocates of 'technical' approaches in professional acting (see chapter 3) believe that their approach is superior to 'method' acting. As one author on the subject put it, 'Olivier could not possibly feel Othello's full passion every night over a three-year run; it would probably kill him'.[25] Certainly, it might prevent him from concentrating on the moves, gestures, voice tones etc which he needs to choreograph with the rest of the cast. Similarly, in order that the nurse or doctor does not let their emotional response impair their clinical judgement, nor spend the bulk of their working life in distress, they learn the art of 'detached concern' whereby they can appear concerned whilst remaining emotionally aloof. The following case studies illustrate this benefit of emotional labour performance:

Case study 1

'In my work [as a probation officer], it is very difficult for me not to get emotionally involved. My emotions come into play in a number of ways – firstly, if I feel disgust or horror about the criminal's crime, then I just can't work with him. So, I have to prevent myself from even thinking about what he did to get himself inside. But, then again, once I hear his story – and the chances are he will have come from broken home with no family support and may even have been abused – it's hard again not to get really involved and take on his case with a passion. I used to do that and I'd come home and still be thinking about how to help him. Or, I'd get terribly upset and take it as a personal insult if he reoffended. Now, I stay a bit more distant and make the right noises and faces without getting quite so involved emotionally.'

Case study 2

'I work in an AIDS hospital and people ask me how I can work in such a miserable setting where people are dying. But, it's not like that – it can actually be quite a cheery place as anyone working in a hospice will tell you. Obviously, it is hard not to feel for the patients and yes, the chances are that they will die. Some of them are amazing people with everything to live for and so much to give society – that is so sad. But I have to distance myself or I would always be sad and mournful. When I first lost patients, I used to come home and be depressed and think, "what a waste". Every time someone died, I would wonder what the point of it all was. But, you learn pretty quickly to stop feeling . . . well, just to stop feeling, I guess. I still care, but I can switch it off now when I go home. You have to.'

In order to act whilst emotionally distancing themselves, emotional labourers can use a number of techniques. One technique is called *cognitive appraisal* which allows the actor to consider the event in terms of rational processes instead of emotional ones. An example of this is given with the debt collectors discussed earlier who are urged not to think of the debtors as nice people but rather as a 'bill you've got to collect'.[12] If they can think of them in these cool rational terms, rather than as real people with their own problems, it becomes easier to put on the angry or tough act necessary to elicit the owed money. More will be said on cognitive appraisals in chapter 8.

There is, another, rather interesting benefit that can occur when workers perform emotional labour. It is thought by some scientists that the act of smiling, even when it is faked, can actually cause the smiler to feel happier. Smiling and laughing involve the contraction of a muscle called the zygomatic muscle which increases the flow of blood to the brain. One scientist likened this increased blood flow to 'taking an oxygen bath'[26] which creates a feeling of happiness. Frowning, on the other hand, is thought to lower skin temperature and electrical resistance so that we feel less happy. These physical changes in our bodies occur even when we might be expected to feel an opposite emotion. For instance, if we were to put a smile on our face whilst looking at a picture of the Ku Klux Klan in action, we would still feel more cheerful than if we did not smile. Similarly, if we frowned whilst watching children play, we would feel less happy than we would without the frown.[25] This is why one researcher said that 'people tend to feel the emotions consistent with the facial expressions they adopt and have trouble feeling emotions inconsistent with these poses'.[27] This is taken on board by some companies – for instance, Mary Kay cosmetic consultants are advised that if they do not feel enthusiastic about the products they are selling then they should 'act enthusiastic and [they] will become enthusiastic'.[4] That is, they should 'offer fake enthusiasm until it becomes a genuine feeling'.[12]

The following case studies illustrate the effects that acting can have on feeling:

Case study 1
'They say that if you have a laugh, you will feel better, don't they? Sometimes, when I am having really tough day at work, I'll go and have a chat with a colleague who always makes me laugh. That always cheers me up! I don't know why, because my problems are still there when I go back to my desk, but it's like the act of laughing convinces my brain that I must be happy!'

Case study 2

'Occasionally at work I feel like scowling instead of smiling. I don't have any contact with customers, so I don't really have to smile a lot. But it wouldn't be considered very nice if I went around with a big scowl on my face – although some people do! I find, though, that if I give a big grin and a cheery "hello", to the secretaries, receptionists, colleagues in the corridor etc, it lifts my spirits temporarily.'

PROBLEMS OF EMOTIONAL LABOUR PERFORMANCE

The problem with emotional labour is that it has some very serious downsides. It can have very damaging consequences for the actor or labourer who can suffer from what I call the 'Have a Nice Day' syndrome. This will be discussed in detail in the next chapter. This section will focus on the downside of emotional labour performance to the *target* of the act.

The main downside of emotional labour for the person who is on the receiving end of the act is that it can appear false and phony, in which case the efforts that the actor has gone to can backfire. Many people dislike phony displays, at least 40 per cent, according to my findings outlined in chapter 2. Many researchers believe that people can tell when an emotion is faked; one points out that 'faking . . . and the mere politeness of a polite smile are often detected'[28] whilst in Egon Ronay's 1980 *Lucas Guide* to the airline companies, the author points out that passengers are 'quick to detect strained or forced smiles'.[2] Consider the following case studies as further evidence of the problem with the fakeness of emotional labour:

Case study 1
'I hate it when I see a store assistant or whatever and they are full of smiles and beams – until you point out that you have a problem. Suddenly, their smile vanishes – quicker than a genuine smile would fade – and they are not interested any more. It's so fake. I'd rather they looked miserable in the first place – then I wouldn't waste my time in approaching them.'

Case study 2
'I work with someone who is so fake. He pretends to be really interested in you and about your problems or concerns. He is always saying that we must go for a drink or get together with our partners, but nothing ever materializes. Sometimes I don't see him for weeks – he works in a different department – then it's all smiles and friendliness. If he was so caring, why doesn't he drop me an e-mail to see how this problem

went or such a thing? When I see him, he often has forgotten what I was even bothered about last time. All his concern is just fake. I wonder if it's a coincidence that he used to be an actor?'

The dislike of phoniness is discussed more in chapter 2, but the next chapter goes on to discuss some more serious problem that chronic or long-term performance of emotional labour can have on the health of the actor.

CHAPTER 6

'THE HAVE A NICE DAY' SYNDROME

'The psychological costs of emotional labour rise sharply when the waitress begins to hate her work and the people she serves and when the telephone operator's care and concern are directed at people whom she finds irritating to the extreme.'[1]

'The great majority of us are required to live a life of constant, systematic duplicity. Your health is bound to be affected if, day after day, you say the opposite of what you feel, if you grovel before what you dislike and rejoice at what brings you nothing but misfortune.'
Boris Pasternak, *Doctor Zhivago*[2]

'This job demand, unique to occupations involving emotional labor, can be viewed as one source of job-related stress'[3]

'When rules about how we feel and how to express feeling are set by management, when workers have weaker rights to courtesy than customers do, when deep and surface acting are forms of labor to be sold, and when private capacities for empathy and warmth are put to corporate uses, what happens to the way a person relates to her feelings?'[4]

All these quotes, from scholars and movies etc. go some way to illustrating the problem that chronic performance of emotional labour can bring to the individual. People who perform emotional labour a great deal of time in their work may suffer from what I term the 'Have a Nice Day' syndrome (HAND syndrome, for short). This syndrome is made up of various different dimensions or components, but the result is that people who suffer from the HAND syndrome may well be:

- Less satisfied with their job.

- More likely to leave their job.

- More likely to take time off work.

- More likely to suffer from minor illnesses like colds.

- More likely to suffer from burnout.

- May even have an increased susceptibility to serious conditions like coronary heart disease.

In order to discover how the syndrome can have all these potentially serious effects, we need to examine the various components of the 'Have a Nice Day' syndrome – or, what can happen if we perform too much emotional labour at work . . .

THE PSYCHOLOGICAL EFFECT OF DISSONANCE

I talked in chapter 5 about emotional dissonance which occurs when the emotions we display (because they are expected) are different from those that we really feel. This is the basis of emotional labour perform-ance. What I didn't mention, however, are the psychological effects that this dissonance can have on people. One scholar puts it succinctly when he says that 'keeping the customer happy does not necessarily imply that the employee herself is happy'.[5] The dissonance that is experi-enced when our displayed emotions do not match our real feelings creates a mental strain.

Psychologists have discovered that this is because when we have two beliefs or attitudes that are inconsistent with each other, we expe-rience a psychological state of discomfort or strain.[6] For example, sup-pose that Joe is a smoker. He is likely to have (at least) two inconsistent attitudes/beliefs about his smoking habit. On the one hand, he enjoys smoking. This is the first attitude or belief. On the other hand, he has been told that smoking is harmful – his second attitude/belief. If he was to simply accept the first belief, that smoking is enjoyable, on its own, there would be no problem and no dissonance experienced. He could happily continue to smoke. If he were just to accept the second belief on its own, that smoking was harmful, then again there would be no dis-sonance and he would simply stop smoking so as not to damage his health. Holding both the beliefs in his mind is much more of a strain because it means that as he smokes, he must face the harsh fact that he is killing himself. With this knowledge, it just does not make sense to continue to smoke. Yet, he and many others like him do continue to smoke, even though they know that it is harmful to their health. Because their continuing to smoke means that they are holding two inconsistent attitudes (ie that they are enjoying their smoke even though it is harmful) then the psychological strain of the dissonance develops.

How is Joe (and millions like him) to reduce this uncomfortable strain of dissonance? There are two main options: either getting rid of the first belief, or the second. He could get rid of the first belief by quitting smoking. Or he could carry on smoking, but get rid of the second belief. This is the option chosen by many smokers; they get rid of the second belief by convincing themselves that smoking isn't really that harmful, or that they don't really care if they knock a few years off their life, and anyway, didn't Uncle Albert, a forty-a-day man, live until 85? By thinking these thoughts, they reduce the strength of the second belief (that smoking is harmful) and thus can continue to smoke without being in an uncomfortable state of dissonance.

This dissonance can occur in other aspects of everyday life. Imagine that Jack, this time, buys a new mobile phone. He has done his research and has selected the best possible model. It has all the features he needs – a large memory capacity, a slim-line set, a long battery life etc. He is very pleased with his purchase, which cost a great deal of money. He gets it home and uses it for a fortnight (the trial period) and is very pleased with it. Then, his friend Jill turns up at his house and shows him her new phone. This one has just come onto the market last week and seems even better than Jack's! It has an even longer battery life, displays the names of callers, has free voicemail etc. At first Jack is devastated. He has paid all that money and it looks like he made the wrong choice.

Jack's two beliefs that cause him dissonance are that (1) he paid a lot of money and (2) maybe he made a mistake. The strain that this dissonance causes is unbearable, so one belief has to change. He can't change the fact that he paid a lot of money, so the only way to reduce the uncomfortable strain is to change his belief that maybe he made a mistake. He does this by coming up with all sorts of reasons as to why his machine is really better than Jill's after all. Such reasons might be – 'who needs so much phone memory anyway – mine is more than enough', 'maybe I do have to pay for voicemail, but it will hardly cost very much – and anyway, I get free calls at the weekend', 'Jill's may be slimmer, but mine is more stylish' etc, until he convinces himself that he did make the right choice. Now, he is no longer in dissonance and the strain is gone. He can relax!

This dissonance, then, can create a similar strain when we perform emotional labour. Here, the two inconsistent beliefs are that (1) I am smiling and (2) I don't feel like smiling. The strain can lead to the emotional labourer feeling false and hypocritical. A vivid example of this is given by the behaviour of a tele-marketer, quoted in the *Wall Street Journal*: when he was called a 'son of a bitch' by a customer, he clenched his teeth and replied, 'Thank you very much, you have a nice day!'[7]

The problem with emotional dissonance is that the strain cannot easily be reduced. In theory, it can be reduced by either changing the emotions that you are displaying, or by changing how you really feel. Neither of these options is very feasible; if you work hard to change the way you feel, perhaps using some of the deep acting skills discussed in chapter 3, then your feelings will be dictated by the organization. Some people feel that this gives their company control over something much more integral to their identity than their emotional display – their heart. For example, consider this case study:

Case study

'I work in a customer service role, and I am expected to be nice and friendly all the time, even when customers are rude to me – which they often are, since I work in an airport at a check-in desk and they are always complaining about things over which I have no control. You know, like baggage allowance, seating allocation etc. Or, if the plane is delayed, they take it out on me. But I have to smile sweetly all the time. It's often just an act, but now we are told that customers don't like phony smiles and we have to really mean it! Well, I object. The company may be able to control my face, but they are not going to control what's inside. They don't own me. This isn't 1984 – they can't employ thought police. I will think what I like. If I was to really try and feel happy when I am being abused, what does that make me?'

The problem is that deep acting all the time can alter the sense of who we are – our identity. As the airline rep above says, 'What does that make me?' if she has to really feel the emotions she is expected to display? It is likely to make her feel that *she* is not in control of her own feelings – her company is. And that is not a comfortable feeling at all. By letting the company control her feeling, she feels that she would lose all sense of who she really is. The company is not only robbing[8] her of her right to display the emotions that she would like to, but even to feel genuine emotion. This is why one researcher who studied the airline industry was led to observe drily, 'surely the flight attendant's sense that "she should feel cheery" does more to promote profit for United than to enhance her own well-being?'[9] This researcher went further by comparing the physical exploitation of a child labourer in the 19th century with that of the emotional exploitation of a flight attendant in the 20th century which, she said, can lead to drug use, excessive drinking, headaches, absenteeism and sexual dysfunction.

This comparison of emotional labour with physical labour has been made by others too. For instance, a British author who studied emotional dissonance amongst nurses commented that 'emotional labour can be as exhausting as physical labour',[10] whilst some US researchers stated that the only difference between physical and emotional labour is that 'manual laborers must bend their body to the task, but emotional laborers must surrender their heart'.[11]

If changing the way we feel in order to reduce emotional dissonance is not the best option, then the only other option is to stop displaying the emotions that are not really felt. This is emotional deviance (see chapter 5) and is likely to result in demotion or even in being fired. As one source points out, the release of real feelings 'may cost the wayward worker a job'.[12]

So reducing the dissonance is problematic, which means that the chances are that people who perform emotional labour a lot in their jobs are likely to be suffering a great deal from the strain of emotive dissonance. Ultimately, such dissonance can lead to poor self-esteem as the worker begins to think badly of the acting that they are doing on a daily basis. For instance, flight attendants studied in the 1980s were continually fighting against the crime of appearing phony which was seen not merely as 'poor acting', but as 'evidence of a personal moral flaw, almost a stigma'.[4]

This lowered self-esteem can lead to depression and cynicism.[13] So much so, in fact, that one researcher argues that since 'putting on an act regularly can be exhausting', emotional labourers should receive 'hypocrisy pay' to compensate for the burden.[14] Indeed, I am told that in Israel there exists a compensation system called 'shame pay' that is given to those workers who regularly have to deal with emotionally charged situations.

Emotional burnout

Other aspects of the 'Have a Nice Day' syndrome include emotional burnout. Burnout is a term that people tend to use a lot (eg 'I'm so burned out') but in psychology terms, it is actually a unique type of stress reaction that is made up of three distinct components.[15] It is also particularly common amongst individuals who do 'people work'. The three components are emotional exhaustion, depersonalization and diminished personal accomplishment.

Emotional exhaustion

This first component of emotional burnout is central to the phenomenon and occurs when individuals are so emotionally drained that they can no longer perform their job effectively. They no longer care or feel for the people that they interact with. Or, according to the scholar who first proposed the concept of burnout, emotional exhaustion is characterized by a 'loss of feeling and concern, a loss of trust, a loss of interest, a loss of spirit'.[16] This is illustrated well by the following case study:

Case study

Nick is a clinical psychologist whose job involves working with up to seven patients each day and spending an hour with each one. He has been working in this job for ten years. He says:

'I feel absolutely drained by the end of each day. With every patient, hour after hour, I have to listen to their particular problem. It's more than that, though – I have to empathize, show understanding, concern, laugh when appropriate and not laugh when it's inappropriate. By now, I have heard every possible problem known to man. There is nothing new, it's the same stuff over and over again. I used to really feel for my patients, feel their pain and suffering. But, you can't maintain this over ten years, day after day. Now, I find it difficult to even care about them. By the end of the day, it's worse. And Friday afternoon is the worst of the lot. I am just not interested any more in the people I see. I don't care any more.'

Depersonalization

This second aspect of burnout occurs when individuals who are emotionally exhausted respond by *dehumanizing* their customers, clients or colleagues. In other words, they stop seeing them as people with feelings and needs, but rather as numbers to be processed, cases or problems. This is seen frequently when employees are heard to refer to clients etc as a number – as in 'do you have the notes for 5681?' – or case – as in 'I had a really difficult appendix today'. The following examples demonstrate this clearly:

Case study 1

'When we first start in medical school, we see patients as people with individual problems and circumstances. So, there would be a patient with a bowel disorder, another person with a hernia etc. Now, I rarely refer to patients in such terms. I, and my colleagues, are more likely to refer to them as "the hernia", "the broken leg" etc. So, I might ask the nurse to administer a pain killer to "the broken leg in bed six". It's terrible when I think about it, like the leg doesn't belong to a real person. But we don't have time to think of patients in terms of people – we can't interact or anything. We just see them in terms of a part to be fixed.'

Doctor

Case study 2

'Every member of staff here has a staff number. I hate being a number. When I ring up Personnel, or Accounts to query something, the first question they snap at me is "what's your number?". What's the point in having a name, if we just become faceless and nameless numbers? I always try and make them see me as a human, a real person, by going to see them in person. They still ask me what number I am, but at least they can see that I am a flesh and blood human and that when they mess up my expense claims, I react as a human. They screw up a lot, and normally, they don't care – I'm sure their attitude is to do with their seeing us a numbers, not people.'

University lecturer

Diminished personal accomplishment

The third element of burnout occurs when individuals no longer see the work they do as being of value, or seeing anything they do as any kind of accomplishment. People who used to get a sense of satisfaction from completing a piece of work no longer get any sense of achievement. It is as if their senses are dulled and they become blind to their accomplishments. The following case studies demonstrate this:

Case study

When I first started in this job, I used to get a real high every time I won a commission or contract for work. These used to be few and far between, and I used to feel really pleased when I got one. Then, seeing my name in print used to give me such a buzz and sense of achievement. It's what I always dreamed of. Then, I would get my name in even more important publications, you know, national high-brow press. But, recently, I seem to be taking it all for granted. I just don't get any buzz any more. It's like, yeah, so, I've got another big piece out, big deal. It just doesn't seem to be impressive any more. I don't get excited.'

Freelance journalist

These three components, then, make up the unique type of stress reaction termed burnout that is associated with the 'Have a Nice Day' syndrome. Burnout itself has been shown to be related to serious negative consequences such as:

• Deterioration in the quality of service offered by employees

• Higher intentions to leave the job

• Actual quitting of jobs

• High absenteeism

• Low morale

• Sleeping problems such as insomnia

• Increased use of alcohol and drugs

• Marital and family problems[15]

THE EFFECT OF EMOTIONAL LABOUR ON HEALTH

Research has identified a number of other potential negative effects on health that chronic emotional labour requirements can increase susceptibility to. It should be stressed here that these effects of health are symptomatic of the 'Have a Nice Day' syndrome, which implies a chronic or continual need to perform emotional labour at work. People who just perform emotional labour occasionally are not thought to suffer from the HAND syndrome, and thus are not as likely to be susceptible to the serious effects on health that will be outlined in this section.

As early as 1959, the ability to 'self-disclose'[17] was linked to a healthy personality. That is, it was thought that those of us who were able to express our true feelings were more likely to be healthy. Neurotic and psychotic symptoms were seen by some as being the barrier that people put up to protect their real feelings and self from the outside world. From Freud to the present, 'bottled-up emotions' have been blamed for physical and psychological symptoms.[18] For instance, people who continually inhibit their emotions have been found to be more prone to disease that those who are able to express their emotions more freely.[19,20,21,22] Typically, the inhibition or suppression of emotion has been associated with an increase in the activity of nerves in the brain and spinal cord and, when this occurs frequently, can increase the susceptibility to disease.[23]

Modern researchers who study the immune system have found a link between the parts of the brain that are responsible for the feeling of emotion and the body's immune system. For instance, the chemical messengers that operate the most extensively in the immune system have also been found to be those that are involved in the regulation of emotion.[24] This suggests that there could be a direct physical pathway allowing emotions to affect the immune system directly. The latest research has even shown that there could be physical contact points between the ends of nerves and cells of the immune system; these physical contact points allow the nerve cells, when emotionally aroused, to release chemicals that affect immunity. In addition, it is thought that hormones released during emotional arousal can directly inhibit the performance of immune cells.[24]

This link between immunity and emotional arousal goes some way to explaining the link thought to exist between stress and disease. When we are stressed, we are emotionally aroused (with feelings such as anxiety, worry, fear etc) and this impairs our immunity. We then become susceptible to minor illnesses such as colds and flu (see next section for more on stress). But an inability to express emotion may also put us at risk from more serious conditions such as cancer onset and progression. One research study into this link concluded that the strongest psychological predictor of cancer is an inability to express negative emotion.[25] This is encapsulated in the rather funny line from the Woody Allen movie *Manhattan*, when Allen's girlfriend, played by Diane Keaton, breaks off their relationship so she can get together with his best friend. Allen responds without emotion and Keaton complains, 'Why don't you get angry so that we can have it out, so that we can get it in the open?' Allen responds with, 'I don't get angry. I have a tendency to internalize. I grow tumors instead'.[26] This may be based on some truth, as the authors on a book on the cancer-prone personality point out that 'a life-long tendency to repress anger and other negative emotions may be one factor that gradually weakens our biological defense against cancer'.[26]

I should stress here that no one is saying that people who suffer from the 'Have a Nice Day' syndrome are going to get cancer. The research merely suggests that people who perform emotional labour frequently may increase their risk quotient. There are obviously many other factors that contribute to cancer onset and progression and readers should not be under the impression that emotional labour performers are at higher risk than, for example, smokers.

In recent years, there have been reports too of an association between the inhibition of anger and hostility with hypertension and coronary heart disease,[27,28,29,30] and this may be due to the fact that attempting to suppress emotions can lead to increased blood pressure.[24]

It should be noted that it is not the lack of emotional expression *per se* that contributes to disease. Rather, it is the 'lack of emotional expression coupled with the desire to express emotion that is (literally) the fatal combination'.[31] This is, of course, precisely what happens during performance of emotional labour.

EMOTIONAL LABOUR AND STRESS

Stress and emotional labour have long been thought to be associated. For example, one study of police officers[32] suggested that the need to suppress emotions at work might lead to increased stress. In other words, performing emotional labour at work is thought to be stressful, especially if it is a chronic or continual problem. My own research into emotional labour performance suggests that the more emotional labour experienced, the more stressed the individual employee is likely to be.[33] Moreover, I also found that the more emotion was hidden during a particular communication, the more that individual claimed that they felt 'strained'.[33] The following case studies provide real-life anecdotes that support this link:

Case study 1
'I don't really know why, but I find it very stressful not being able to show my real feelings. I have to put a lot of mental energy into

controlling the emotions I display. That would be OK if I didn't also have to use mental energy on a million and one other things. If I was an actor, it would be fine, as that would be my job. As it is, it's just a nuisance that gets in the way of the real work. It's mentally draining and stressful. As if I don't have enough stress at work, without this.'

Case study 2

'It is a strain having to think so much about your facial expression, body language etc. But, more than that, it is stressful not being able to let your real feelings out. For example, if I have a row with my boyfriend, I find that a good shouting match releases all my pent-up anger! If we argue, then he storms off in a huff, I am left with all my feelings inside. They build and build until he comes back – and then I let rip! But at work, it just builds and builds and there's just no outlet. It is definitely stressful.'

Stress, often thought to be the scourge of modern society, is a thoroughly *unmodern* phenomenon. It is, in fact, a perfectly normal reaction that would have been a lifesaver for our ancestors. Stress then was a physical reaction that would have provided them with a means of drawing on extra reserves of strength and energy so that they could escape from their predators. Thus, stress was an *adaptive* response that helped humans adapt and survive in their environment by providing special surges of energy with which to either flee from danger or stay and fight. A psychologist called Cannon, in 1935, first came up with the idea of stress being the 'fight or flight' mechanism that we hear about so often today. In other words, Cannon postulated that stress is a reaction that occurs in our bodies in order to prepare us to fight our enemies or run away and escape. Of course, today the things that cause us stress are not predators, but deadlines, work overload, job insecurity and emotional labour. These are on-going stressors and, when we look at the mechanisms of the stress response, we can begin to see how being continually stressed can affect our health.

Hormones are the main protagonists in the stress reaction and when we are stressed, they are released from our adrenal glands (near the pancreas) into the bloodstream. They have one main goal: to prepare the body for fight or flight. Both fighting and fleeing require the ability to have extra strength in the arms and legs and more energy in the muscles. The aim is thus to divert as much oxygen- (and thus energy-) carrying blood as possible to the arm and leg muscles from other parts of the body. To do this, the body stops concentrating on non-essential functions like digestion that can wait until later. Blood is thus diverted from the stomach, skin and internal organs to other more important areas where it can contribute to the pressing need to fight or flee.

Adrenaline is one hormone that is often mentioned and this, when released from the adrenal glands to the bloodstream, results in a faster heart rate and raised blood pressure as the heart works harder to pump blood around the body. Cortisol is another hormone released from the adrenal glands and its job is to act on the liver to convert protein to glucose (sugar), which is a major source of energy. This glucose thus provides the energy for blood to be pumped faster and allows us to be able to run or fight with extra strength.

Another vital set of chemicals is released from the hypothalamus in the brain. These are endorphins and they act as natural pain-killers so that we feel less pain to stop us being distracted from the urgent task of fighting or fleeing. This is why footballers and athletes are able to continue playing with broken bones, and why our ancestors could still run after a chunk of their arm had been eaten – the endorphins delay the pain response until a more convenient time.

All these reactions were ideal for a real 'fight or flight' situation. If we are faced with a mugger in the street or an angry Rottweiler, the stress reaction that occurs prepares us well. But this reaction is not so good for continual stresses at work that will not respond too well to us either running away or clobbering the source of our stress on the head (especially if the source of stress is the boss!). Clearly, what was a great adaptive response to threat early in our evolutionary history is not much use when faced with the modern stresses of the 20th and 21st centuries.

In fact, the situation is a lot worse than that. Not only is the old stress reaction practically useless in most work situations, it can actually be harmful and there are both short-and long-term effects that will be discussed in turn:

Short-term effects
The problem in the short-term is that we have all this extra glucose surging through our muscles, and no opportunity to use this extra energy. This can result in a whole range of commonly experienced symptoms. For instance, one of the first symptoms of stress is a 'tension headache', which is the result of a continuous surge of blood to the brain – whilst this enables us to think more clearly in the short term,

after a while is can lead to headaches. Headaches can also be caused by tensing of the neck muscles, which we tend to do when we are stressed – of course, this can lead to a stiff neck too.

Another common sign of stress is feeling perpetually tired. The stress reaction allows us access to special reserves of energy, but when they are used up, we can feel exhausted. It is vital that we replenish our energy stores by eating healthily, but, invariably, stressed people have no time for such things, and they rely on junk food or quick short-term energy bursts from chocolate or snacks.

Another short-term effect of stress is stomach ache or stomach upset (such as indigestion, cramps, diarrhoea or constipation). This occurs because blood is diverted away from the stomach area during the stress reaction so it can flow to the limbs and brain. This means that the digestive mechanisms are reduced which can lead to digestive problems and discomfort.

Finally, we might experience dizzy spells when we are stressed. Although we may breathe more quickly when we are stressed, we tend to take more shallow breaths and thus we do not breathe in as much oxygen as deeply as when we are not stressed. This can lead to a slightly reduced supply to the brain, causing dizziness.

Long-term effects

When we remain stressed for long periods of time, or our stress levels rise very frequently, we may experience more serious effects. For instance, stress causes our blood pressure to rise as the heart works harder at pumping blood around the body more quickly. This can lead to the condition of hypertension or raised blood pressure, which can contribute to coronary heart disease as the heart struggles to cope with the increased demands on it (of course, there are other physical factors involved too, such as the presence of cholesterol which blocks the arteries).

Poor digestion can eventually lead to stomach ulcers whilst stress can also result in a general lowering of the immune response, making the stressed individual much more vulnerable to illness – this is why stressed people tend to get colds and flu more frequently and why they often take longer to recover when they do get them.

Stress is thought to be a factor contributing to many other conditions such as allergies (eg allergic asthma which is thought to be exacerbated by stress or emotional arousal), skin rashes (caused by the continuous reduced blood flow to these areas or stress-related changes in skin cells[34]) and diabetes (stress and the stress-related stimulation of blood sugar is implicated in the onset and cause of certain types of diabetes in those people who are predisposed to it – stress may thus trigger a dormant condition.[34])

If emotional labour is stressful, as I and previous researchers (to say nothing of many of the people suffering from emotional labour) believe, then it is not difficult to see how emotional labour and the 'Have a Nice Day' syndrome can pose quite serious threats to the health of the labourer. This is perhaps why recent articles in the press about my research have carried headlines such as 'Have a nice day but remember I'm dying' (*The Australian*, 8 January 1998), 'Health risk to staff who say: "Have a nice day"' (*The Times*, 7 January 1998), 'Why being nice at work could make you ill' (*Zest* magazine, 1 March 1997), and 'Phony smile at work will end in tears' (*Daily Mail*, 8 January 1997).

WHO IS MOST AT RISK FROM THE 'HAVE A NICE DAY' SYNDROME?

Not all researchers are of the view that it is inevitable that people performing emotional labour will suffer from the 'Have a Nice Day' syndrome. There are thought to be some conditions or circumstances that make some people more 'immune' to the syndrome than others. The reverse side of this is that there are equally some people who are *more* at risk from the syndrome than others. For instance, workers who are at more risk from the full effects of the syndrome include those who:

- Are in high 'people-centred' jobs.
- Are in jobs that are in the public eye.
- Are in jobs that are especially emotionally demanding.
- Have less personal control over the way they work.
- Are naturally less attentive to social cues that tell us how to behave.
- Have no outlet outside work for their real feelings.

Each of these categories will be discussed in turn.

High 'people-centred' jobs
It would seem understandable that workers whose jobs entail them having continual and repeated contact with other people are likely to suffer

from 'people fatigue', a symptom of the 'Have a Nice Day' syndrome. Such workers include those working in:

- Customer care
- Call centres
- Managerial positions
- Reception areas
- Enquiry desks
- Patient care
- Teaching

Although the above list in not exhaustive, it does cover those workers who are most at risk from the syndrome because their jobs are people-centred. These workers spend a large proportion of their day interacting with other people, whether they be customers, clients, patients or colleagues, and whether on the phone or face-to-face. When individuals spend more than 60 per cent of their day in contact with people, the chances are that they are having to manage and control their emotions most of the time, without any real opportunity for release. Very often too, they will be expected to switch from one kind of emotional display to another as they switch their dealings from person to person.

Jobs in the public eye
There are a number of people whose jobs means that they are continually working under public scrutiny. The pressure for these people is not just that they can rarely show their true feelings whilst working – the extra stress comes from the severe consequences that can result if their real feelings should 'leak out'. Such jobs in the public eye include:

- Politicians
- TV presenters
- Celebrities
- The Royal Family
- Company directors
- Public relations workers

Most of these jobs, by their very nature, entail some degree or other of emotional control. Consider the politician who is asked, on peak-time television, his or her opinion of a new government policy that they find abhorrent. Or the television presenters for a morning television show who detest each other but who must present a friendly façade to the public. Or the celebrities who are married and who must suppress any signs of the huge row they have had before opening a garden fête. Or the member of the Royal Household who must attempt to hide his or her disgust for the exotic dish they have just been served with. The list of possibilities is endless but in all cases, leakage of real feeling could be catastrophic. Governments could fall, entire countries could be offended and jobs lost over a leakage *faux pas*. Thus, these people are at more risk from the serious effects of the 'Have a Nice Day' syndrome.

Emotionally demanding jobs

By 'emotionally demanding' I am referring to those jobs where the emotional climate is highly charged. In other words, strong emotions are frequently present within the work environment – but the worker is not able to express these strong emotions as others around him or her are. The most common group of workers in these environments are nurses and doctors who must work with people who are terribly sad, distressed or in great pain. The worker may feel some of these emotions too, but must work hard at suppressing them in order to present an appropriate mask.

It is likely that workers who must suppress or manage strong emotions may suffer more from the effects of the 'Have a Nice Day' syndrome than people who must only suppress mild emotion. Thus, it is probably easier to suppress a mild dislike of someone than it is to suppress strong feelings of horror on seeing a badly mutilated patient.

Low autonomy jobs

Workers who must perform emotional labour according to a very rigid script are probably likely to suffer more from the effects of the 'Have a Nice Day' syndrome than those who have more freedom to behave within any particular emotional culture. That is, it is perfectly possible to have a 'Have a Nice Day' culture that does not have an inflexible 'fast-food server' script; in these cases, workers are under a general expectation to perform in a certain emotional way, but are given some autonomy and freedom with the words and behaviours they choose. Many such cultures, however, do have very tight scripts and deviations are not condoned. Such workers typically include:

- Fast-food workers

- Hotel receptionists

- Telephone operators

- Sales representatives

- Time-share dealers

I include the last category, time-share dealers, because of the following case study:

Case study

'I was in Florida and was approached by a time-share company. The deal was that if we sat through a ninety-minute presentation, we would get tickets to one of the theme parks for less than a quarter of their price. So we went, but were determined not to fall for any of the sales patter. Because we had both worked in sales, we had the perfect technique to unsettle our rep. We knew that he would have a strict script, so our challenge was to get him out of his script! For instance, when he began by showing us pictures of his family, we turned away and showed our disinterest clearly. If he had been clever, he would have responded and moved on, but he did not dare deviate from his script, so he ploughed on. He later told us about all the great activities that were available at the time-share apartments – karaoke and bingo etc. I told him that I hate that sort of thing and that he was really putting me off by telling me about them. But, instead of switching tack, he just started to get sweaty and red, but carried on telling us! He grew more and more uncomfortable and stressed but could not deviate from his script.'

In this case the worker with the script has no autonomy over how he behaves or over the emotions he displays. This time-share rep could not use his freedom and discretion and so the stress is likely to be far more severe. If the rep had been allowed to switch tack, whilst still being warm and friendly, he might have experienced fewer visible signs of stress. To put it crudely, workers who can choose to say 'have a nice day' or 'have a great day' can have more control over their emotional behaviour and, even though they are still working in a particular emotional culture with the expectations that this has, they may be likely to experience less associated stress.

All the above factors discussed are related to the conditions of the job of the worker, and to that extent are external or outside of the individual make-up of the employee. The factors that follow, however, are to do with the personality or characteristics of the individual and are, to a large degree, unrelated to or independent of the job itself.

Low 'self-monitoring' workers

'Self-monitoring' is the extent to which people observe and control the image that they present of themselves in any social situation. The person who first described self-monitoring, Snyder, says:

> 'Some people are particularly sensitive to how they appear in social situations – at parties, job interviews, professional meetings – in circumstances of all kinds where they might be motivated to create and maintain an appearance. These people carefully observe their own performances and skilfully adjust their behavior to convey the desired image, acting like different people depending on the situation and their audience. It is as if they are actors for whom life itself is a drama in which they play a series of roles, choosing the self that best fits the circumstance at hand'[35]

What Snyder, an American psychologist, noticed was that people vary in the extent to which they are able to monitor their own and other people's emotional expressions. People who are very good at 'self-monitoring' are able to monitor or control the image of themselves that they wish to project. This is impression management and high self-monitors are thought to be particularly good at managing the impression they create by paying careful attention to the emotions that their culture expects them to display. Such people need no script or formal display rules – they are able to read the emotional culture of an organization and know how to behave.

Low self-monitors, on the other hand, are not very concerned with assessing the social climate around them for rules and expectations. They remain largely oblivious to their emotional surroundings and simply do not pick up upon the display rules and expectations unless they are given a script or formal rules. The following table shows the differences between high and low self-monitors:

High self-monitors . . .	Low self-monitors . . .
Are strongly concerned about whether their behaviour is appropriate.	Do not worry too much about whether their behaviour is socially acceptable.
Are very attentive to the behaviour of others in order to decide how to behave themselves.	Behave according to how they feel and disregard the behaviour of others as a cue to their own behaviour.
Are very good at modifying and controlling their emotional expressions.	Are not as good at emotion management because it is not as important to them.
Use impression management very frequently and in many situations.	Rarely use impression management – what you see is what you get with low self-monitors.
Often behave differently in different situations.	Usually behave similarly in different situations since their behaviour is based on how they feel, not how they ought to behave.

High self-monitors, then, are highly sensitive to what is expected of them and are thus much more likely to be comfortable following display rules and displaying the right emotions for the emotional culture that they are in. After all, they are well used to adapting their emotional display according to the situation – emotion and impression management is second nature to them. High self-monitors then, are not as likely to suffer from the 'Have a Nice Day' syndrome as low self-monitors. For low self-monitors, monitoring their social environment in order to decide how to behave does not come naturally. These people do not engage in much emotion management, preferring to be honest about how they feel. The pressure of conforming to expectation and display rules at work is thus likely to hit them harder.[3] In addition, it is likely to be much more exhausting for low self-monitors to start controlling their emotions than for high self-monitors who are more used to it, as the following two case studies go some way to demonstrating:

Case study 1

'I am very much the sort of person who is open and straightforward. What you see is what you get. I don't go for airs and graces in order to impress people. I don't lie – I am totally honest. If I like something, I say so. If I don't, I'll say so too. You always know you are going to get the truth from me. It's not always popular – in fact, some people don't like it one bit. I am not the sort to ask people how they are if I don't care and people think that's rude, but I don't care. I once worked in a job in an hotel where I was expected to do all the "how do you do" stuff, but I couldn't hack it. It just wasn't me. It felt false and hypocritical. And it was bloody hard work thinking about how I was meant to behave, when I was meant to smile all the time!'

Case study 2

'I think that I care very much about what other people think of me. I am always thinking, what do they think, do they like me? I will always try and make a good impression by, I don't know, agreeing with them, smiling, nodding etc. It just helps make a good impression. My job needs that too, and it is just an extension of what I normally do. It isn't too difficult because I always put on a kind of mask anyway. Well, not really a mask, more of a costume. Yes, I put on a different costume according to who I am speaking to.'

People with no outlet for their emotions

Some people are more susceptible to the 'Have a Nice Day' syndrome, not because of the demands of their job or their personality type, but because of the fact that they have no opportunity to let their real feelings out. Many people who manage and control their emotions all day at work either come home to a 'second shift' of emotional labour[9] whereby they are expected to manage their emotions in front of their spouse or children, or else they simply have no one to talk to about their day. People in these categories include those who:

- Have a partner at home who is emotionally demanding.

- Have a partner at home who has an emotionally demanding day.

- Have a partner at home who also performs a great deal of emotional labour at work.

- Have children.

- Are single.

- Have a lot of evening activities that are 'people-centred' such as meetings, or socials.

People who have a 'second shift' of emotional labour are those who are likely to work hard at managing their emotions all day at work and come home exhausted. Instead of being able to relax or tell their partner about their day, they are expected to listen to their spouse's bad day, discipline the kids, listen to demanding friends or tearful relations etc. In other words, their emotion management shift is not over yet. Without that release, the stress builds more and more. Similarly, single people who may not have someone to release their emotions with (some do, of course, whilst many non-single people do not) can be particularly susceptible to the ill-effects of the syndrome.

One group of people who could be at risk are those who go out a lot on dates or to meet new people in the evenings. Whilst meeting new people can be a very pleasurable activity, it can also be stressful in that we all tend to manage our emotions and perform emotional labour to some degree with new people. When we are doing this straight from a hard day of emotional labouring, the results can be particularly exhausting.[36]

Case study 1

'I spend my day in stressful situations, dealing with people who are hurt or upset. I have to offer comfort and assurance whilst not getting too involved. Sometimes I feel like crying, but I bottle it all up until the end of the day. Then I go home, but have to deal with the kids playing up or whatever. Even if they are being good, I don't always feel like showing interest in their little pictures or their day. Sometimes, when they show me a drawing, I just want to say – what a load of rubbish! But, I have to pretend to be impressed and pleased – it's hard work. My husband is a nurse too and he is usually the first to off-load all his emotional baggage – by the time I've listened to him and pretended to care, I am too exhausted to speak. That is my life.'

Nurse

Case study 2

'I joined a dating agency recently and have been going on about two or three dates each week with different people. I love it – it's very exciting. But it is also very draining after a hard day's work. You have to appear enthusiastic and interested in yet another sob story or life history – I work as a counsellor, so have enough of this at work. It's exhausting – I just wish sometimes that I could go home and be myself.'

Single Male

This then concludes the chapter on the 'Have a Nice Day' syndrome. Of course, the real question now is, what can we do to reduce or cope with the syndrome? Chapter 8 will outline some effective strategies, but first, let us examine in chapter 7 some facts regarding the degree to which the syndrome is a problem in everyday life at work.

CHAPTER 7

OUR SECRET EMOTIONAL LIVES AT WORK

In this chapter, I am going to present the first-ever study that has shown the emotions that we commonly feel, fake and hide during our everyday lives at work. This study was carried out by monitoring over 550 workplace conversations and allows, for the first time, a real insight into our secret emotional lives at work. After this, there will be an opportunity to see how *you* compare to other people – you will be able to complete the same questionnaire that I used in the study to assess your own emotional labour performance. This will enable you to see if you are likely to suffer from the 'Have a Nice Day' syndrome and will be invaluable when reading chapter 8, which discusses the best strategies for coping with the effects of the syndrome. But first, that unique insight into the secret emotional life of people around us . . .

HOW MUCH EMOTIONAL LABOUR DO WE REALLY PERFORM AT WORK?

The discussion of emotional labour in the previous chapters is all very well, but how much emotional labour is really performed at work? Is it really as big a problem or phenomenon as I am making out? According to my findings, the answer is an unequivocal 'yes'! My study shows that *three quarters* of all communications or conversations at work involve the employee performing some emotional labour, whilst in a third of conversations, people reported performing *substantial* amounts of emotional labour.[1] This means that in three out of every four conversations at work, people are likely to be either faking emotions that they do not really feel, or hiding emotions that they do feel. They are doing this because of the presence of display rules and expectations from the customer or employer (see later section in this chapter).

Is this good or bad? Well, on the one hand, all the benefits of emotional labour performance that were discussed in chapter 5 are likely to accrue if people are faking appropriate emotional displays and hiding inappropriate ones. Thus, in all likelihood, customer loyalty will be improved, stores will sell more products, staff will get more tips or commission, employees will get on better with colleagues and generally the world is probably a much nicer place because of the emotional control that people are exhibiting.

On the other hand, if we are performing emotional labour in three quarters of all our communications at work, the possibilities for suffering from the 'Have a Nice Day' syndrome are wide-ranging. The syndrome is likely to be a big problem at work – possibly bigger than previously thought. Certainly, this study showed that there was a relationship between stress and emotional labour performance such that the more emotional labour performed, the more stressed the individual said they felt.[1]

Because no psychologists or researchers have attempted to measure emotional labour before, we have no way of knowing whether this figure of three quarters is higher or lower than, say, a decade ago, before emotional labour performance is thought to have become so commonplace (because of the reasons outlined in chapter 2). The only suggestion that emotional labour performance has grown comes from a guess from one researcher in 1983 that 'roughly one third of American workers today have jobs that subject them to substantial demands for emotional labor'.[2] Although this estimate coincides with the present finding that one third do indeed experience substantial levels of emotional labour, if we consider performance of emotional labour *per se* the current findings (of three quarters of all communications involving some degree of emotional labour) suggest the presence of emotional labour is a lot higher than previously thought. It could well be that emotional labour requirements have indeed grown over the years (although the 1983 researcher gave no estimate of general levels of emotional labour – only substantial levels), as the comments in chapter 2 suggest. That is, the proliferation of many similar products means that in the service industry, companies are having to rely more and more on emotional display to differentiate their product from that of another company. Away from the service industry, as we become more and more insecure in today's climate of downsizing, delayering and redundancies, we are having to rely more and more on displaying the appropriate emotions such as enthusiasm and interest in order to secure and keep our jobs. All these situations are likely to call upon emotional labour performance.

The answer to the question of whether the amount of emotional labour we perform at work is a bad thing or not is provided by delving a bit deeper into the findings of my research. Other than the link between emotional labour and stress that I found, there seems to be one other potential negative consequence of emotional labour performance that has not really been thought about before; people who perform significant amounts of emotional labour during communications at work are more likely to consider that those communications are not as successful as those that do not involve performance of emotional labour.[1] In other words, when we are faking emotions a great deal or hiding how we really feel, we somehow think that the outcome of the conversation will not be as successful as it would be if we could display our real feelings.

Why should this be? The following case study may shed some light on this success–emotional labour relationship:

Case study

'When I am smiling and being nice and friendly when I don't really mean it, I imagine that the other person must guess or be able to tell that I am faking it. I can usually tell when the smiles are false so why shouldn't they? And, if they can tell, then surely the conversation won't be successful – certainly if we mean in terms of, say, that person liking me, agreeing with me, being happy with my explanation or the service I am offering. No, I don't think a conversation that isn't honest can be successful, unless you are a very good actor.'

If this is true, then the implications about emotional labour performance are even more far-reaching than previously thought. Emotional labour, it seems, may not only have a detrimental effect on health as described in chapter 6, but could also affect the success of the performance. If we are performing emotional labour in three quarters of all our conversations at work, does this mean that we are only likely to have successful outcomes in a quarter of our transactions? If this were true, then should we all, employees and managers alike, take immediate measures to reduce or cope with our emotional labour performance? (Some such measures will be outlined in chapter 8.)

Another interesting finding about our secret emotional life at work is that people in positions of power and authority are less likely to perform emotional labour than people lower down the career ladder.[1] This is probably because the more power and authority we have, the less we need care about what other people think. When we are the 'big boss' our job is less dependent on the impression we create and we have less need to care about smiling and being friendly. As we climb the career ladder, our freedom to display the emotions we really feel grows – which means that our susceptibility to the 'Have a Nice Day' syndrome should *decrease*. Certainly, it is hard to imagine that the boss of a huge multinational company, or even a smaller one, need be concerned with saying 'have a nice day' too much. As one source puts it, 'the dominant . . . have relative freedom from emotional constraints in organizational life'.[3]

For the rest of us, the demand to manage our emotions continues. We can only dream of the day we no longer need be concerned with display rules, but in the meantime, if we are ever to reach such echelons, we must continue to control how we feel – or at least how we *appear* to feel.

WHICH EMOTIONS DO WE TEND TO HIDE AT WORK?

In 60 per cent of all the communications I monitored, people claimed that they did indeed hide emotion. The most commonly suppressed emotion is anger, which is hidden in 10 per cent of all communications. After that, the most suppressed emotions were anxiety, disappointment, dismay and boredom.[1]

That anger is the most commonly hidden emotion is, perhaps, not too much of a surprise. It is a very strong and intense emotion and, as such, is one that we are not very often at liberty to express. We are more likely to be free to express mild disappointment than we are the intense passion of anger. Displays of anger in the workplace are very much frowned upon, as the following case study demonstrates:[4]

Case study
Vanessa lost her temper with her boss and ended up losing her job too. She says:

'My boyfriend had dumped me for someone else and I was really feeling angry. I had been fed up with my boss's chauvinistic attitude for a while and one day I really let rip, telling him exactly what I thought of him in front of other staff and customers.'

Vanessa received a verbal warning but as the incident occurred during her probationary period, the area manager decided that she should have her contract terminated.

My finding that anger is the most commonly suppressed emotion should ring alarm bells for you if you are frequently hiding your own feelings of anger (if you are not sure, fill in the survey at the end of this chapter). The problem is that anger suppression is linked to serious conditions like hypertension (raised blood pressure) and coronary heart disease, as pointed out in chapter 6. Not only is this worrying for the individual who is having to hide his or her feelings, but it should also be a concern for the employer who may have to deal with sickness and absenteeism years down the line. And, who knows, will workers start suing their employers for making them perform too much emotional labour? After all, there are many cases of people suing their employer for putting them at danger from physical conditions. If emotional labour is harmful, and the employer knows this, why should they not be sued too?

Boredom at work is another emotion that has been highlighted by my study, but is very much overlooked by most employers. According to one eminent Australian expert in emotion, 'nearly everyone experiences episodes of boredom at work from time to time'[5] and my findings suggest that this could indeed be a widespread problem. Suppressing boredom is probably not as harmful as suppressing anger, but, when combined with having to fake interest and enthusiasm, could certainly contribute to the 'Have a Nice Day' syndrome.

Why are emotions suppressed at work? Is it because the person we are talking to has said or done something that angers or bores us? Or is it because we are just having a bad day or have personal problems or worries that are distracting us? When I delved deeper into the results of this unique study, I found that about half of the negative emotions hidden (such as anger, anxiety, boredom, disappointment or dismay) were feelings that were already present before the conversation.[1] In other words, these were pre-existing emotions that might have been caused by a previous conversation, something that may have happened at work, an upsetting letter received at home, a row with a spouse etc. This lends considerable credence to the idea discussed in chapter 1 of the 'overcoat theory of emotion' in which I propose that emotions do 'leak' and that we cannot just leave them to one side as we can with our overcoats.

The evidence here that we are having to cope with 'leftover' emotions in at least a fifth of all our interactions at work (and in half of the interactions in which emotions are hidden) provides strong support for this theory. Clearly, we, and our managers, need to acknowledge that emotions are not overcoats – they stay with us all the time.

Which emotions do we express – and fake – at work?

Emotions are expressed at work even more than they are hidden. We tend to express some kind of emotion in nearly all our workplace communications – 92 per cent to be exact. The most commonly expressed emotion is interest, which is expressed in nearly half of all the communications I monitored. Enthusiasm is expressed in a third of communications at work, with other emotions such as disappointment, dismay, sympathy and happiness expressed rather less.[1]

That enthusiasm is expressed so much is no great surprise to emotions researchers such as myself. The literature is crammed with anecdotal evidence that shows how much enthusiasm in valued at work. In fact, if there is any one emotion that I would advise readers to display, it would indeed be enthusiasm. As the magazine *Cosmopolitan* recently said, 'Smiling and being enthusiastic are vital but underestimated tools for getting on at work'.[6] Look at these examples of how real companies place so much value on enthusiasm:

- Mary Kay cosmetic consultants take a 'vow of enthusiasm'.[7]

- DHL Worldwide Express aims to create an 'environment that rewards . . . enthusiasm'.[8]

- Apple's Macintosh team were seeking employees who could demonstrate 'exaggerated enthusiasm'.[6]

- McDonald's look for 'desirable traits . . . such as enthusiasm'.[9]

- Continental Airlines want staff who 'convey a spirit of enthusiasm'.[2]

- Delta Airlines expect their employees to display to a 'steady level of enthusiasm'.[1]

So, employers want employees to express enthusiasm, and, indeed, my findings show that employees are expressing enthusiasm. But how much of this enthusiasm is fake? The answer seems to be, quite a lot. At least a third of expressed *positive* emotions such as enthusiasm or interest are fake. This means that the next time someone appears really enthusiastic about something you are telling them, there is a one in three chance that they are faking it! Far less *negative* emotion, however, is faked (only a tenth of negative emotions are faked). Thus, if anger is expressed at work, there is a very good chance that it is genuine.

Which is the more stressful, faking emotion that we do not feel, or hiding emotion that we do feel? This interesting question was addressed by examining the relationships between faking and suppressing emotion with simple measures of stress. The results suggest that it is harder to *suppress* negative emotions than it is to *fake* them. But, when it comes to positive emotions, it is the other way around – it's harder to *fake* positive emotions than it is to *suppress* them.

☹	More work in *suppressing* **negative** emotions (eg anger, disappointment)	☺	Less work in *suppressing* **positive** emotions (eg joy, enthusiasm)
☹	More work in *faking* **positive** emotions (eg joy, enthusiasm)	☺	Less work in *faking* **negative** emotions (eg anger, disappointment)

The comments in the following case studies go some way to helping us understand why this might be:

Case study 1

'When I am having to hide emotions such as disgust or anger from patients, or even doctors, I find that much harder than when I have to hide, say, happiness because I have just got a promotion or won a few quid on the Lottery. Why should that be? I think maybe the anger or disgust is more powerful. Maybe if I won a million pounds on the Lottery, my joy would be so powerful that hiding that would be hard too!'

Nurse

Case study 2

'I often have to fake a whole range of emotions. You want to know which I find easiest to fake? I can pretend to be disappointed about something quite easily – if a customer is disappointed with a product, I can pretend to share their disappointment too. But if a colleague got promoted, I would find it harder to share their joy. Maybe that's because I am a jealous so-and-so and my envy makes it harder for me!'

Customer Service Manager

IS THERE ANY EVIDENCE THAT DISPLAY RULES EXIST AT WORK?

This study of 550 communications at work shows that employees are very much aware of the existence of display rules. In over half of the conversations, people claimed that they had either laughed or frowned, not because they genuinely felt like doing so, but because it was expected of them.[1] In other words, the rules governing their emotional display were so strong that they found themselves displaying physical expressions of emotion simply because they were expected. We all do this at times, of course. We might laugh at jokes that are not funny or frown to show an empathy that we do not really have. Every time we do this, we are conforming to a display rule. The fact that this study shows that at work we do this so frequently – in every other conversation – suggests that the emotional labour requirements produced by display rules are indeed high.

Furthermore, in at least 80 per cent of conversations, people felt that they were somehow 'putting on a face' that did not reflect their true feeling at all.[1] That is, they arranged their faces so as to display certain emotions – but not emotions that were naturally felt. Again, this is strong evidence that display rules are alive and kicking throughout organizational life. As if more evidence was needed, in the same number of conversations, people were able to acknowledge the presence of rules that governed how they should speak and act. The following case studies illustrate the point:

Case study 1

'I am aware that there are rules about how I speak at work. The rules aren't written down anywhere, but everyone knows them. For instance, there is a rule that says we shouldn't yawn in front of a customer – it's common sense in a way, but it's still an unwritten rule. We aren't meant to be human at all in front of customers – no eating, drinking, chewing or any other human act. We should smile sweetly at all times. No one says this, but the customer might say, "Oh, you're nice and friendly", which makes us do it even more.'

Case study 2

'I speak very differently at work than out of work. My kids call it my work voice. It is more posh – more refined and proper. You know, I don't say "yeah" and I pronounce all the letters. I smile a lot and look interested and enthralled. When I come home, that's it, I'm not faking it any more!'

WHAT IS YOUR SECRET EMOTIONAL LIFE LIKE?

Clearly, the results of my study presented in this chapter suggest that many of us are performing a great deal of emotional labour, whether by faking emotion, suppressing it or conforming to display rules. People who are performing emotional labour this much are likely to be susceptible to the consequences of the 'Have a Nice Day' syndrome as outlined in the last chapter. The real question, of course, is, how do *you* compare to the rest of the population? Are you at as much risk from the syndrome as everyone else – or maybe you are at less, or even more risk?

To help you find out, I am making available for the first time to the public the Mann Emotion Requirements Inventory, or MERI™ for short. You can use the MERI™ to work out how much emotional labour you perform, on average, in your day-to-day working life. Here's how it works. The MERI™ should be taken to work with you and completed after conversations you have with one other person, whether they be customers, clients, bosses, subordinates or colleagues. After each conversation, you need to take a minute to complete a MERI™, which asks you a series of questions about your emotions during the encounter. Ideally, you should complete a MERI™ after at least five, and preferably ten conversations that you have at work – and the best thing is if they are the next five or ten conversations you have.*

* MERI™ is copyrighted © Copyright 1999 by Sandi Mann and Ward Dutton Partnership. This means that there are restrictions on photocopying it. Further copies, together with a response pack, and, if required, a personal profile of your results, are available from Ward Dutton Partnership, Hill Farmhouse, Chishill Rd, Heydon, Nr Royston, Herts, SG8 8PW, UK. Tel 01763 837111.

MERI™
(Mann Emotion Requirements Inventory)

For most of the following questions you are asked to indicate how much you agree with each statement by circling the appropriate point on the scale. For example, if you strongly agree with the statement 'I felt confused during the encounter' you might circle 1 or 2 as follows:

Agree   *1*   *2*   *3*   *4*   *5*   *6*   *7*   *8*   Disagree

1 How much during the encounter did you hide (or try to hide) some kind of emotion from the other person?

A lot   *1*   *2*   *3*   *4*   *5*   *6*   *7*   *8*   None at all

2 Because of events in my personal life or at work, I felt negative (eg depressed, upset, angry, frustrated) BEFORE this encounter, but felt that I had to try to hide my feelings and put on a 'brave' face to the other person.

Agree   *1*   *2*   *3*   *4*   *5*   *6*   *7*   *8*   Disagree

3 Because of events in my personal life or at work, I felt positive (eg excited, happy, proud) BEFORE this encounter, but felt that I had to try to hide (or tone down) my feelings from the other person.

Agree   *1*   *2*   *3*   *4*   *5*   *6*   *7*   *8*   Disagree

4 During the encounter, I felt that I was 'acting' a role or taking on a role such as helper, advisor, expert, teacher, parent, counsellor or boss.

Agree   *1*   *2*   *3*   *4*   *5*   *6*   *7*   *8*   Disagree

5 At some point during the encounter I felt that I intentionally conveyed (or attempted to convey) a positive emotion or feeling that I did not really feel but that was appropriate at the time (I pretended to be happy, excited, interested etc).

Agree   *1*   *2*   *3*   *4*   *5*   *6*   *7*   *8*   *Disagree*

6 At some point in the encounter, I felt that I intentionally conveyed or attempted to convey) a negative emotion or feeling that I did not really feel but that was appropriate at the time (eg I pretended to be angry, upset, dismayed etc).

Agree   *1*   *2*   *3*   *4*   *5*   *6*   *7*   *8*   *Disagree*

7 During the encounter I felt that the other person expected me to take on a role such as helper, advisor, expert etc.

Agree   *1*   *2*   *3*   *4*   *5*   *6*   *7*   *8*   *Disagree*

8 I felt that I acted differently in this encounter than I would have done at home or with friends.

Agree   *1*   *2*   *3*   *4*   *5*   *6*   *7*   *8*   *Disagree*

9 I felt a bit 'fake' as if I was not really being 'me' at some point in this encounter.

Agree   *1*   *2*   *3*   *4*   *5*   *6*   *7*   *8*   *Disagree*

10 I felt that I suppressed or hid (or tried to) positive emotions at some point in this encounter (eg I felt happy or excited but tried not to show it).

Agree   *1*   *2*   *3*   *4*   *5*   *6*   *7*   *8*   *Disagree*

11 I felt that I suppressed or hid (or tried to) negative emotions at some point in this encounter (eg I felt angry, depressed or dismayed but I tried not to show it).

Agree   *1*   *2*   *3*   *4*   *5*   *6*   *7*   *8*   *Disagree*

12 I felt that at some point, the other person expected me to have a particular 'face' or disposition (eg they expected me to act friendly, helpful, enthusiastic, cool, emotionless, distant, warm etc).

Agree   1   2   3   4   5   6   7   8   *Disagree*

13 I 'psyched' myself up so that I would genuinely feel any emotion that I was expected to feel (eg the other person was very excited so I tried to work up enthusiasm too).

Agree   1   2   3   4   5   6   7   8   *Disagree*

14 At some point, I laughed or frowned because it was expected rather than because I found something amusing or distressing.

Agree   1   2   3   4   5   6   7   8   *Disagree*

15 At some point I felt stressed or found it a strain because I could not show my true feelings (because it would not have been appropriate).

Agree   1   2   3   4   5   6   7   8   *Disagree*

16 At some point during the encounter I felt stressed or found it a strain because it was difficult to maintain the role that I was taking on.

Agree   1   2   3   4   5   6   7   8   *Disagree*

17 I felt that there were rules or protocol about how I spoke or acted in this encounter (eg my company expects people in my position to behave in a certain way or have a certain manner).

Now, you can work out your MERI™ score which will be between 17 and 136. Add up your scores for each of the 17 items. If you have completed five MERIs™, you will have five scores. Simply add the five scores and divide by five to give an average. If you have ten scores, add them all and divide by ten. So, you should end up with an average emotional labour score which will be between 17 and 136.

Your Emotional Labour Score [ ]

Here is a general indication of what this overall score indicates:

17.................65...................90...................114...........136
Very high emotional labour	**High emotional labour**	**Mild emotional labour**	**Low emotional labour**

Your overall emotional labour score can be compared to those of other people. Most people experience:

- Very high emotional labour (scores of 17–65) in about a tenth of their conversations at work.

- High emotional labour (scores of 66–89) in about a quarter of their conversations at work.

- Mild emotional labour (scores of 90–113) in just over a third of their conversations at work.

- Low emotional labour (scores of 114–136) in just over a quarter of their conversations at work.

☺ If you scored more than 114

This means that on average, you do not perform much emotional labour in your working life. This suggests that you tend to have the sort of job where you are generally free to express the emotions that you really feel whilst you do not really need to hide your true feelings very often. You feel that you can generally be 'yourself' without fear of not fitting in or risking your job. This means one of three things:

1 It may be that your job does not involve much contact with people.

---

2 It could be that your personality is an ideal fit to that of the organization's, ie that the emotions you tend to feel are the ones that your organization tends to expect you to express.

3 Alternatively, it could be that you are expressing the emotions that you feel despite these being inappropriate or undesired by your organization.

The first two options, emotional harmony, are reasonably healthy and mean that emotion management is not a significant source of stress in your work life. If you feel that you *are* stressed, it may be that the significant sources of stress are from elsewhere. A stress management course, stress counsellor or good self-help book will help you identify your particular stressors.

If you are expressing your true feelings even though you know that your organization does not approve of them (eg you are scowling at customers), then it is likely that your personality is not an ideal fit to the job role. This is emotional deviance. You may be feeling dissatisfied with your job, stressed because you know that you are constantly flouting rules or protocol and maybe even insecure because you may lose your job. It may be worth thinking about leaving your current job to find something more suited to your emotional personality.

It may be that you have some areas that may be sources of emotional labour to you and you can identify these by comparing your scores on the individual MERI™ items in the next section.

☺ If you scored more than 90 but less than 114

Your result shows that you do experience mild levels of emotional labour in your work life. This means that you are sometimes having to fake emotions that you do not feel and/or suppress emotions that you do feel. Your job probably involves some contact with people.

This is a reasonably healthy state to be in. It is quite natural that we fake emotions sometimes and hide our true feelings. After all, social acting is an important social skill that helps us get on with other people. It may be that you generally enjoy your job and suit your job role but that sometimes you are bored, disinterested, distracted by personal problems or by mundane matters such as your shopping list! This is perfectly reasonable and as long as your emotional labour levels remain in this band, you have nothing to be concerned about.

However, it might be worth examining your scores across the individual MERI™ items (see next section) to see if there are any areas that are more emotionally demanding for you than others.

☺ If you scored less than 90

You generally experience high levels of emotional labour in your working life. This means that you are frequently having to fake emotions that you do not really feel whilst hiding those emotions that you do feel. You may have a job that demands a great deal of contact with people, perhaps with customers, and that involves your taking on a role that is not the 'real' you.

This is a fairly unhealthy state to be in and suggests that emotional labour for you is a significant source of workplace stress. You are likely to feel tired and emotionally drained by the end of your day. In the long term, this is likely to cause you stress and the symptoms shown in the table in the last chapter may result.

In order to reduce the stress associated with your emotional labour performance, you must take preventative action. Suggested techniques and strategies will be demonstrated in chapter 8. The point to remember is that you should not simply stop performing emotional labour. That is, you should not now suddenly start displaying your true feelings! That is likely to lose you your job since your work role clearly depends on you taking on roles, managing your emotions and acting where necessary. Instead, the answer is to reduce the stress associated with your emotional labour performance.

In order to help you identify which areas are the most significant sources of emotional labour to you, compare your scores across each of the individual MERI™ items with those of the rest of the population (see next section).

Identifying specific sources of emotional stress

You will also have a score of between 1 and 8 for each of the 17 MERI™ items. This section will enable you to see how your score compares with those of other people. For example, if the average score for Item 1 for the rest of the population was 4.5, and your average score is 6, then this means that you experience the source of emotional labour defined in Item 1 LESS than the average. If your score was 2, then you experience this source of emotional labour MORE than the average. Use this section to identify your specific areas of emotional stress.

For each of the 17 items, you need to work out an average score. So, if you completed five MERIs™, you will have five different scores for each item. You will need to add up each of the five scores for Item 1 and divide by five to get the average. You will need to do this for each of the 17 items. Now, write the average score for each of the 17 items in the boxes below.

When you fill in the boxes with your scores, circle those that are *smaller* than the average score as in the example below:

8 Because of prior events, I felt positive before this encounter but had to try to hide these feelings.	6.9	4

Then you will be able to see all the areas where you experience emotional labour MORE than the rest of the population.

MERI™ Item	Average score of population	Your score
1 During the encounter, how much did you hide some kind of emotion?	5.9	

What your score means: If your score is less than the average then you tend to hide more emotion than the rest of the population. This could be because you have personal problems outside work, you are feeling stressed or worried, or that you rarely feel the emotions that you are expected to display at work. You are often in a state of emotional dissonance. This means that you are more at risk from the HAND syndrome than most. The opposite is true if your score is higher than the average.

MERI™ Item	Average score of population	Your score
2 Because of prior events, I felt negative before this encounter but had to try to hide these feelings.	6.7	

What your score means: This item is to do with how much we carry negative feelings with us to work. If your score on this is lower than the average, then you tend to carry more emotional baggage with you to work. This suggests that you are either going through a tough time at the moment and have personal problems, or that you are simply not happy in your job. If your score is very much lower than the average, then it might be worthwhile seeking help or taking time off work.

If, on the other hand, your score is higher than the average, then you are relatively free of emotional baggage and are able to leave any negative feelings at home when you go to work (emotional harmony). It could also mean, however, that you simply do not hide your negative emotions at work, in which case you may be in a state of emotional deviance. If this is the case, and you are expressing emotions such as sadness, misery or dismay, then you should be aware that other people may 'catch' your emotions and you will not be too popular with the boss! At the risk of increasing your susceptibility to the HAND syndrome, you may want to hide your negative feelings more (but read the strategies in the next chapter to ensure that you don't suffer too much from the HAND syndrome).

MERI™ Item	Average score of population	Your score
3 Because of prior events, I felt positive before this encounter but had to try to hide these feelings.	6.9	

What your score means: If your score is lower than the average, then this means that you are frequently having to hide positive feelings like happiness, joy or enthusiasm. It could be that you work in a 'Have a Cool Day' culture or even a 'Have a Rotten Day' culture and this is why you are constantly having to suppress your naturally cheerful self. Remember, suppressing positive emotions can be stressful too. On the other hand, your positive feelings may just be temporary – it could be that you have just had some good news over the past few days which is causing you to feel unusually happy!

MERI™ Item	Average score of population	Your score
4 During the encounter I felt I was acting a role.	4.7	☐

What your score means: Feeling that you are acting a role is not unusual and most of the population that I surveyed felt this at some point during the communications they monitored. If your score is below the average, then this means that you are (or at least, you feel that you are) acting a role quite substantially. This could cause you problems in your identity and self-esteem as you begin to wonder who you really are. You could experience feelings of being phoney and this could affect your self-esteem. Turn to chapter 8 for strategies on dealing with this.

If your score is higher than 4.7, then this means that you do not feel like you are acting a role as much as the rest of the population. This could be good – it could mean that you feel naturally capable in your work role with no need to act. However, most people have to take on roles to some extent at work, and if your score is very high, you might want to consider whether you could do more to create or maintain the role in which you are employed. Do other people give you the appropriate respect, do you get the appropriate responsibility etc? If not, it could be that you need to act more appropriately for your role sometimes.

MERI™ Item	Average score of population	Your score
5 I faked a positive emotion.	5.5	☐

What your score means: Again, most people I surveyed agreed that they did, to some extent, fake positive emotion (such as enthusiasm, interest, friendliness etc) during the transactions monitored. This is because most of us work in a 'Have a Nice Day' culture that requires these positive emotions to be displayed. If your score is less than 5.5 this means that you fake 'Have a Nice Day' emotions a great deal. You may work in a service culture but certainly in a 'Have a Nice Day' culture. If your score on Item 11 is also less than the average, then you are the most at risk from the HAND syndrome.

If your score is more than 5.5, then the chances are that either you are a naturally cheerful soul, or you work in a 'Have a Cool Day' or 'Have a Rotten Day' culture. Any of these situations is healthy. If, however, you are indeed working in a 'Have a Nice Day' culture but you don't express any expected positive emotions (emotional deviance) then you are in danger of losing your job!

MERI™ Item	Average score of population	Your score
6 I faked a negative emotion.	7	

What your score means: Few people in my survey felt that they had to fake negative emotions like anger or dismay. Generally, when we express such emotions, it is because we really feel them. If your score is much less than 7, then it could be that you are one of the relatively rare people who work in a 'Have a Rotten Day' culture. If you also have a low score on Item 10, you could be at significant risk of suffering the HAND syndrome.

MERI™ Item	Average score of population	Your score
7 I felt the other person expected me to take on a role.	4.2	

What your score means: Again, feeling that there is an expectation to take on a role, such as counsellor, teacher or student, is quite common at work. When we are explaining things or having things explained to us, for instance, we take on the appropriate role. If your score is less than 4.2, then you clearly do this rather more than other people and this could be something to do with the nature of your job – you may be a training manager, a therapist, or in any job that requires taking on the persona of a particular role. If you also have low scores in Items 4, 8 and 9, then you are likely to be at risk from the HAND syndrome.

If your score was much higher than 4.2, then this means that you did not feel that there were any expectations for you to take on a role. This is quite unusual, since most of us have some expectation that we take on a role. It could be that you really are able to be 'yourself' at work, or it could be that you are not engaging in enough appropriate role-suitable behaviours (see comments for Item 4).

MERI™ Item	Average score of population	Your score
8 I acted differently than I would have elsewhere.	4.6	

What your score means: It is quite normal to feel that you are generally acting differently at work than you would, say, at home or with friends. Thus, if your score is around the 4 mark, this would be normal compared with the rest of the population. If your score is less than 3, this suggests that you feel that you are very much different at work from the 'real you'. If you also have low scores on Items 4 and 9, then you could be at risk of feeling that you just cannot be 'yourself' at work or that the self you present at work is widely different from the self you present elsewhere. This could mean that you are not entirely well-suited to the work environment that you are in – perhaps you should be looking for a more suitable job that will allow you to be a little truer to yourself. Alternatively, you could use the strategies outlined in chapter 8 to cope with the symptoms of the HAND syndrome that you may be experiencing.

MERI™ Item	Average score of population	Your score
9 I felt 'fake'.	6	

What your score means: Most of us evaluate being 'fake' in a negative way, which could explain why the average score on this was quite high. If your score is less than 6, this could be quite normal too, since if we are taking on roles and managing emotions at work, we are likely to feel a bit 'fake'. If your score is below 3 on this item, then you could be feeling quite bad about what you might see as your phoniness. The best situation at work is obviously when we do not feel fake most of the time, so if you do, you should look at the coping strategies outlined in chapter 8 or think about an alternative job.

MERI™ Item	Average score of population	Your score
10 I hid positive emotions.	7	

What your score means: It is relatively rare to have the need to have positive emotions that occur during a communication at work. For instance, if we are given good news or shown something exciting, it is usually perfectly acceptable to display such feelings. If your score is much lower than 7, it could be that you work in a 'Have a Cool Day' culture in which any kind of emotional expression is frowned upon. This can be quite stressful although not, perhaps, as stressful as having to hide negative emotions. If you have a low score on this item, but you don't work in a 'Have a Cool Day' culture, it could be that you are a fairly emotional person and that you often feel extremely positive about things – as mentioned earlier, displays of extreme or intense emotion are rarely encouraged at work.

MERI™ Item	Average score of population	Your score
11 I hid negative emotions.	5.8	

What your score means: It is far more common to have to hide negative emotions such as anger, boredom or dismay than positive ones – and probably more stressful too. If your score on this item is less than 5, then it is likely that you are not especially happy in your job at the moment. It could be that you disagree fundamentally with the views or expectations of your boss or colleagues, or that you are feeling stressed or unhappy about some aspect of your work or non-work life. On the other hand, it could be that you work in a customer service post and you are constantly having to hide your negative reactions to customers – you might even be suffering from verbal abuse or bullying at work (in which case, you might want to search for alternative employment). Chapter 8 will give you tips on coping with the problems of having to hide your real feelings.

MERI™ Item	Average score of population	Your score
12 I felt the other person expected me to have a particular 'face'.	4.2	☐

What your score means: This question is one of the items dealing with display rules or expectations that other people (customers, colleagues, the boss etc) have of the emotions that you display. Most people are aware that they have to put on a certain 'face' at work – a compassionate one, a caring one, understanding etc. If your score on this item is less than 4, it could be that you put on a face more than most in which case you may work in a culture with very strong display rules. You are likely to suffer more from the HAND syndrome than people who only feel that they have to put on a 'face' some of the time.

MERI™ Item	Average score of population	Your score
13 I 'psyched' myself up to feel an expected emotion.	6.7	☐

What your score means: This item measures the degree to which you generally perform deep acting at work (see chapter 4). Deep acting is when we try and work ourselves up to really feel the emotion we are expected to display – as opposed to just plastering that emotion on our face (as in surface acting). We can deep act by 'psyching' ourselves up by trying to instil the required emotion in ourselves. The survey results suggest that this kind of deep acting is not too common and that most people probably surface act rather than deep act. If your score is less than 6, then you are probably different and deep act more. This should have the benefit of reducing the feelings of phoniness and fakeness that surface actors can feel. In other words, people who surface act more are likely to feel more negative about their acting than deep actors. However, deep acting is likely to require more mental effort and as such can be more stressful. It also means that you are actually feeling every emotion that you are expected to, so your work life can end up being an emotional roller-coaster, compared to surface actors who just pretend to feel every emotion.

MERI™ Item	Average score of population	Your score
14 I laughed or frowned because it was expected.	6.2	

What your score means: This item measures the physical parts of emotional display and is concerned with how much we physically display emotion on our faces. Low scores on this item suggest that you are having to put a great deal of physical energy into your emotion management since laughing continually when you don't mean it can be exhausting.

MERI™ Item	Average score of population	Your score
15 I found it a strain not being able to show my true feelings.	6.1	

What your score means: If you scored less than 6 on this item, then you are already only too aware of how stressful it is to have to manage your emotions. The lower your score on this item, the more likely it is that you are suffering from the HAND syndrome. The strategies in chapter 8 will teach you how to reduce the strain associated with emotion management at work.

MERI™ Item	Average score of population	Your score
16 I found it a strain maintaining the role.	6.5	

What your score means: This is a slightly different item than 15 and refers more to the strain of maintaining the role of counsellor, teacher, advisor etc, than actual emotion management. Some people can take on roles without too much stress, but others find it stressful. If your score on this item is less than 6, it could be that the role you are taking on does not feel comfortable or is at odds with your values or beliefs. For example, a gentle person who has to take on the role of disciplinarian might find it more stressful than a more forceful person. Thus, if you have a very low score on this item, you might need to think about whether you can take on roles that you are more comfortable with.

MERI™ Item	Average score of population	Your score
17 There were rules or protocol governing how I acted.	3.7	☐

What your score means: This item is a direct measure of the degree to which display rules exist in your organizational culture. The average score is very low, which means that very few of us exist in cultures where display rules do not exist. Most of us have to contend with quite obvious display rules that govern how we talk or act. If your score is higher than 5, then you are probably in a much freer climate where the rules are not so apparent. Scores over 6 indicate that you could be quite senior in your organization and thus don't need to obey such rules.

Now that you have been able to identify specific sources of emotional stress and have a good idea about the degree to which you perform emotional labour in your work (and thus, the degree to which you may be susceptible to the 'Have a Nice Day' syndrome'), you are ready to start working on ways to cope with emotional labour and the syndrome. The next chapter will present a range of techniques that you can adapt to your own particular circumstances.

CHAPTER 8

COPING STRATEGIES FOR THE
'HAVE A NICE DAY' SYNDROME

It's all very well learning that you perform emotional labour a great deal at work or that you may be susceptible to the HAND syndrome, but is there anything that you can really do about it? Surely, being nice at work is part of the job and if we suffer from ill-effects, well, that's just an occupational hazard? This is certainly the view of many people – managers who don't want to take responsibility for the problem, and workers who feel helpless about it. We should not forget that not so many years ago, hazards such as losing a limb, being crushed to death or inhaling carcinogenic fumes were all considered to be acceptable health risks that were to be suffered in exchange for the privilege of being able to earn a living. Nowadays, we no longer accept such danger to our physical health, and employers have a duty in most countries to ensure that their workers are not knowingly exposed to physical risk.

Why should things be any different when the risk is to mental health? Especially when that risk is thought to have a knock-on effect on physical health too. It is my belief that it will not be too long before employers will be forced (by lawsuits, if not by the desire to cut absenteeism and turnover costs) to take more responsibility for the emotional labour of their workers. Until that happens, it is up to the individual worker to attempt to cope with the HAND syndrome and the potential negative consequences of the emotional labour they perform. Fortunately, there are a number of strategies that workers (as well as their managers) can employ themselves and these can be grouped into three categories, each of which will be discussed in turn:

> ❑ **'Downtime'**
> ❑ **Calming strategies**
> ❑ **Cognitive restructuring**

'DOWNTIME'

'As with physical labour, after a sustained period of emotional labour, an alternative or rest are necessary.' [1]

Just as there are laws and regulations about how much physical labour workers are allowed to be engaged in without a break, so there ought to be laws and regulations about how much emotional labour workers can be involved in without a break. The concept of 'downtime' [2,3] is to provide a break or time-out from the emotional demands of the job. It does not necessarily mean a break from the job itself, but only from the emotional demands of it. This is very important, since it is inevitable that there will be resistance from management to introducing downtime if they think that this means simply more coffee breaks. In fact, downtime is about structuring the work schedule so that employees work smarter rather than less. Such schedules should, ultimately, increase rather than decrease productivity.

Downtime can be introduced through the following work organization strategies:

- Shift rotation

- Multi-skilling

- Programme scheduling

- Downtime signals

- Real feelings schedules

Shift rotation is where workers, during any particular shift, will rotate high people-contact work and low people-contact work with colleagues. This can be illustrated by the case of a large health insurer in the UK. Their customer service employees spend their entire working day on the phones, dealing directly with the public. The culture is 'Have a Nice Day' and the potential for suffering negatively from emotional labour performance is high. To counteract this risk, management has introduced a shift rotation scheme. Any one worker will rotate through three shifts throughout the day. The first shift is a 'red' shift, whereby any calls from customers will be routed directly to them. People on red shifts are likely to be dealing with customers continuously. After 50 minutes on a red shift, they will rotate onto an orange shift whereby calls are only put through when all the red shift workers are already occupied. In an orange shift, workers can expect calls every five to ten minutes. After another 50 minutes of this, the worker moves into a green shift whereby calls are put through only if all red and orange shift operators are busy. Workers on this shift can go their entire shift without receiving a call. After this downtime, they then move back to a red shift.

During orange and green shifts, workers catch up on paperwork that would otherwise have been completed by a separate team of workers. Thus, the programme is cost-effective to the employer, since workers are achieving more, whilst suffering less burnout. The customer gains, because the operator they call is fresh and interested in them. The only costs to the employer are in terms of start-up and training costs.

Such schemes only work if staff are **multi-skilled**. That is, whereas before the scheme, there were two sets of workers doing different work (paperwork and answering calls), the same workers are now multi-skilled and can do both. Other examples of how multi-skilling can help reduce the HAND syndrome are in fast-food restaurants. Traditionally, the work is divided into cooking, serving and cleaning. Staff are employed to perform one of these three roles. This means that servers are continuously 'customer-facing', ie dealing with the public all the time in a very strong 'Have a Nice Day' culture. By training staff to do all the jobs, the workers could rotate their shifts in the same way as in the red, orange and green shifts in the example above. There are clearly some training costs involved, but these would be negated by the long-term savings in reduced turnover and absenteeism associated with burnout (and boredom!).

Of course, not everyone works in such a rigidly defined environment and many people are able to structure their day themselves. This is where **programme scheduling** can help. This is when a worker makes a conscious decision to build downtime into his or her working day. The following case study illustrates how this can be done:

Case study

Sarah is an internal marketing manager and spends much of her day in meetings. Her work also involves a great deal of writing and designing of such things as newsletters and in-house magazines. Although attending meetings is vital, she had begun to feel that they were getting in the way of the 'real' work of writing and designing and was often impatient and frustrated in meetings. She was frustrated by the lack of progress and by the slow pace of the meetings and she was impatient to get back to her work. She realized that she was experiencing emotional labour every time she stepped into a meeting as she suppressed her boredom, impatience and frustration and pretended to be enthusiastic and interested. Sometimes one meeting would last up to three hours and she often had a day filled with meetings back-to-back.

To cope, Sarah used a programme scheduling strategy whereby she only scheduled a certain number of meetings each day and rarely back-to-back. She ensured that she had downtime between meetings where she did not have to perform emotional labour and where she could get on with her 'real' work. This reduced her feelings of impatience and frustration in meetings since she knew that she would soon be free to pick up her on-going work projects. She also attempted to reduce the time that meetings took and their frequency by sending out any information that could be covered in letters or memos, or having e-mail discussions where possible. This reduced her stress considerably.

The point about downtime is that it is a period free from emotional labour. It will not necessarily eliminate the emotional labour experienced the rest of the time, but should reduce the stress associated with it since there is at least a break when real feelings can be expressed or when feelings need not be faked. Sometimes downtime involves the worker physically moving into a different environment such as coffee areas, cafeteria or the grounds outside. Other times, the worker stays in the same place – thus the green workers in the shift system did not themselves move, but the calls moved away from them. In these instances, a **downtime signal** may be needed to tell the worker that they are now able to express their feelings more openly. In the case of the health insurance workers, such a signal is hardly needed since they must still perform emotional labour each time the phone rings – it just rings less often on some shifts. However, in other kinds of jobs, especially those that are not in the public domain, there may be times when people may be more emotionally honest. For instance, at office parties, Christmas parties or after-work outings, workers may be allowed to be more honest with each other than they can be at work. Thus, staff are allowed to insult their manager in a good-natured manner or ridicule a colleague's dress sense. Emotions tend to run more freely as the alcohol runs, and alcohol can, in these cases, serve as a signal that downtime is beginning.

Professional actors, who are in roles and who must manage their emotions continually in order to perform their work, may manage to avoid the ill-effects of emotional labour by the invariable downtimes that punctuate their work. For example, one actor I spoke to said, 'When I must act angry even though I am feeling quite happy, I can come out of role as soon as the director says "cut" or whatever . . . I can then mess about, have a laugh with colleagues and generally release my true feelings.' For them, the downtime signal is the instruction from the director.

It should be noted that the only true downtime is solo downtime. Any break or time-out that still involves contact with people will not entirely fulfil the purpose since 'off-stage' settings may have their own display rules. For example, the cafeteria may provide a break from customer contact, but spending the entire lunch break with colleagues means that true downtime is not achieved. It is rare not to have to manage emotions to some degree or other even with colleagues, as my own research has shown. The best option is to be sure to take at least ten minutes real 'solo' downtime too. Another option is to introduce **real feelings** schedules. Because it is so rare for workers to be really able to display their true feelings, real feelings schedules give permission for this to happen in a particular place or at a particular time. For instance, the Christmas party mentioned earlier may be a real feelings time when staff can let their true emotions out. Although they are likely to regret it if they tell the boss what they really think of them, there is likely to be more tolerance to real emotions on these occasions than in the normal office environment.

Another way to introduce real feelings schedules is used by some service companies where staff are dealing with customers. Diaries or record sheets are provided in which staff can record incidents that have caused them difficulties. These are often anonymous and provide the opportunity to be really honest and let those pent-up emotions flow, as the following case study demonstrates:

Case study

'We have an incident book that we can write in anonymously, and management are very tolerant of extreme displays of emotion recorded in it. For instance, I was once dealing with a member of the public who demanded the phone number of Head Office. We are not allowed to give the number out at all, so no matter how much she ranted and raged, I could not help her. Actually, I thought she was right – why can't we give the number out? Why should we protect the sensitive little things in Head Office from real customers? I felt really angry during the conversation – angry that I was getting all the flak for enforcing an inane rule. Afterwards, I wrote it in the incident book, and let my anger fly. I was quite insulting about management and this petty policy and was very direct. I think they got the message – and I felt better.'

Calming Strategies

Whilst it can be a very effective strategy for reducing the stress that might result from the chronic performance of emotion management at work, 'downtime' is not always the best approach for everyone. People who might find such a strategy problematic include:

- Those who do not have any control over the type of work they perform at any given time.

- Those whose entire job role involves contact with people and who thus cannot easily incorporate 'downtime' into their daily work life.

- Those with unsympathetic employers who may not take kindly to requests for 'downtime' (of course, if you show them this book, they may well become more sympathetic and may even introduce new work schedules to incorporate 'downtime'!).

For these people, a better approach for coping with the stress caused by emotion management at work might well be learning a few 'calming strategies'. Ideally, these would be used in conjunction with 'downtime' and 'cognitive restructuring' (discussed in the next section), but can also be used effectively on their own. The whole point of calming strategies is that they, quite simply, calm away the pent-up emotion. There are a number of calming tricks that the chronic emotional labourer would do well to keep in his or her 'toolbox' of coping strategies:

Taking a few deep breaths

This is a very simple technique that one employee who frequently performed emotion management as part of her job role referred to as simply 'getting myself together'.[4] When faced with the prospect of having to hide boredom or anger from a customer, fake interest or enthusiasm in a project, or pretend to be sympathetic to a colleague, taking a few deep breaths serves several functions:

- It forces you to stop, acknowledge the fact that you are feeling stressed and gives you a chance to identify why you might be stressed. Self-awareness and identification of sources of stress at work are the keys being able to deal with it successfully.

- When we are stressed we tend to take faster and more shallow breaths which reduces the quality of oxygen reaching our lungs, heart and brain. Breathing deeply performs the physiological function of forcing more oxygen into your lungs, heart and brain. This can have a refreshing effect and provides your vital organs with the energy they need to cope with stressful situations and can also reduce or prevent immediate symptoms of stress such as headaches or muscle pain that are caused by reduced flow of oxygen to these areas. When breathing deeply is combined with relaxation techniques (discussed next) the benefit can be increased further.

Relaxation techniques

The earlier sections of this book (especially chapter 7) should mean that you are well on the way to becoming aware of when you are performing emotional labour at work (ie when you are either faking emotions you do not feel or hiding emotions you do feel, or both). You should also, by now, be well aware that such work or labour is stressful. You may well already experience some symptoms of stress at work such as those discussed in chapter 6.

Relaxation techniques are an ideal method for everyone to use to help reduce the symptoms of stress before they occur. Once you recognize that you are performing emotional labour, then that is the time to think about implementing relaxation strategies. You can wait until you have the symptoms of stress such as a pounding headache, a stiff neck, aching muscles, stomach upset etc, but relaxation is best used as prevention rather than cure.

There are a number of different strategies, ranging from 'quickie' techniques designed to be used whilst you are actually performing emotional labour, through to more in-depth versions that can be used during 'downtime' or in coffee- or lunch-breaks.

◆ 'Quickie' relaxation technique

Next time you feel your anger rising with that rude customer or your unappreciative boss, try this three-step relaxation technique. The beauty of this technique is that no one will even know you are doing it!

☞ Step 1 Clench and unclench the muscles in your hands, arms, legs and buttocks. Very often when we are stressed, we tense these muscles without even noticing. We only realize it when we start to get the aching muscles or headaches.

☞ Step 2 Slow your breathing down by breathing longer deeper breaths (see above). Each time you breathe out, imagine that you are breathing some of your anger (or boredom, frustration or whatever emotion you dare not reveal) away. Some people find it helps to visualize the emotion as a balloon that deflates as you slowly breathe it away.

☞ Step 3 Relax your posture. If you are sitting, slump your shoulders slightly, relax your legs and rest your hands on your lap. If you are standing, take a more 'at ease' stance.

Case study

Jayne, a manager I interviewed for my research, can vouch for the benefit of the 'quickie' relaxation technique. She says:

'I am often in the situation at work where I am involved in on-going control of my emotions. I have to be patient with subordinates when I really want to scream at them for being so stupid! Then I have to be sympathetic to my own boss when he tells me his cash-flow problems – I don't care really, as I have enough of my own problems! Then, I might have a colleague who is excited about a family event – a wedding etc, but I just haven't the time to listen. I have to smile sweetly though and pretend to be interested. At times like this, I just plaster a smile on my face and do a quick relaxation exercise. It refreshes me and allows me to release some of my emotions, and there is no outward sign that I am doing anything other than listening attentively!'

◆ 'Coffee-break' relaxation technique

This is a longer version of the 'quickie' technique and is performed ideally whilst you are sitting comfortably with your eyes closed and will not be disturbed. This is ideal for carrying out at the end of an emotionally draining or stressful day.

☞ Step 1 Starting at your toes, clench and unclench three times. Work your way slowly up your body: your ankles, calf muscles, thighs, buttocks, chest, shoulders, neck, arms and fists. Finally, scrunch up your face and eyes. Learn to really feel the difference between stressed, tight muscles and relaxed, unclenched muscles.

☞ Step 2 Now start slowing your breathing down. Take slower and deeper breaths – imagine your lungs filling with pure energizing oxygen and imagine that oxygen flowing through your veins to your heart and brain. Visualize in your mind a situation in which you have performed emotional labour today. Imagine that during that situation, you were sitting on a large balloon on top of an armchair. The balloon contains all the emotions that you were really feeling. Each time you breathe out, some of the pent-up emotions in the balloon are released and you gradually sink deeper and deeper into the comfy armchair until the balloon is completely empty of any suppressed emotion.

☞ Step 3 Now, keep breathing out slowly, and this time, each breath out should be accompanied by the word 'relax', which you should say in your mind, not aloud.

☞ Step 4 Revisit your scenario (from Step 2) in your mind and see if, when you think of it, you feel as stressed as you did before. If you still feel stressed, go back to Step 2, but this time, imagine that the balloon full of suppressed emotion is a little smaller than before.

☞ Step 5 Once you can think of your scenario without feeling stressed, pick another emotionally draining incident that occurred today, and start with Step 2 with that one. Repeat Step 5 until you have dealt with all the sources of emotional stress that you experienced today.

If you can get into the habit of using the 'coffee-break' relaxation technique regularly, you should really reap the benefit. Your blood pressure is likely to lower, your breathing will become slower and you are less likely to become stressed as easily from emotional labour performance. A quality control manager I interviewed who manages a staff of ten uses this kind of relaxation technique most days:

> 'When I get in from work, I take 10 or 15 minutes to release the day's emotion. I sit in a quiet room and my family know not to disturb me – that's my time. I feel so relaxed and free afterwards and it means that I no longer release my pent-up emotions on my wife, or the cat!'

Deep relaxation techniques

This is a much longer and deeper version of the coffee-break technique and takes about 20–30 minutes. It can be used every night, or whenever you feel especially stressed. The best way for this technique to work is to record the script onto a cassette and play it back. Make sure that you are sitting comfortably and that you will not be disturbed by the phone or by your family.

The Script

'I want you to start by sitting comfortably in your chair or lying down on the bed. I want you to think about the feeling of sitting or lying and to notice how soft the chair feels. Notice the feeling under your feet, legs and back. Feel the fabric under your hands. Close your eyes – not too tight, but nice and relaxed.

'Now, start to think about your breathing. Take a long, slow, deep breath, hold it for a couple of seconds, then breathe out, nice and slowly. Do that again, but this time as you breathe out, I want to you visualize all your pent-up emotions, stress and tension being forced out of your lungs. Breath in. And out. Once more, breath in, and out. Feel the stress being breathed out.

'Now, I want you to think about your toes. Notice the way they feel in your shoes or socks. Now I want you to scrunch your toes up tightly – as tightly as you can without them hurting. Hold them like that for a second – feel the tension in them. And, relax them. Notice the difference between tension, and relaxation. Enjoy the feeling of being relaxed. Now, once again, tense those toes in both feet. And relax them. Don't forget to keep breathing out nice and slowly and every time you are breathing out you are imagining the stress, tension and pent-up emotion being released.

'Now, start thinking about your whole foot. Notice the weight of your foot on whatever surface it is against. Now, scrunch your feet tightly so that they curl in. Hold and feel that tension as your feet are curled so tightly. Hold it . . . and relax them. Feel the difference between tension, and relaxation. Keep breathing in, and out, slowly visualizing all the emotion and stress being expelled from your lungs. Now, once more, tense your feet and really feel that tension. And, let it all go – let all the tension out and enjoy the feeling of your feet being nice and relaxed.

'Your lower leg muscles are next. These are the muscles below your knees. Tense them tightly and hold them there. And, slowly, relax them. Remember, every time you breathe out you are imagining that the stress and tension is being forced from your lungs. You can almost see it being exhaled. Now, once more, tense those lower leg muscles and once more let the tension go. As you let the tension go, breathe out nice and slowly, so that you are letting the emotional tension go too.

'By now you should be starting to feel nice and relaxed. Remember to keep your breathing nice and slow and as you breathe out, every single time, you are breathing out more stress and tension. Every time you breathe out, you are exhaling more and more stress and tension from your body. After every breath out, there is less and less tension left in your body and mind.

'Now we are up to your thigh muscles. Once more, notice how the skin of your thighs feels next to the material of your clothes. Now, take a long slow breath and tense those thigh muscles really tightly. Hold the tension. Feel how uncomfortable it is to have such tension in your thighs. And, re-lax those thigh muscles. Let all the tension go and really enjoy and savour that sensation of being truly relaxed in your thighs. Now, repeat – tense those thigh muscles really tightly – hold it and feel the tension. And, let go, relax. As you breathe out, you are imagining the pent-up emotions being released from your body.

'Now we are up to your stomach muscles. Once more, notice how relaxed your lower body is. Now, take a long slow breath and tense those stomach muscles really tightly. Hold the tension. Feel how uncomfortable it is to have such tension in your stomach. And, re-lax those stomach muscles. Let all the tension go and really enjoy and savour that sensation of being truly relaxed in your stomach. Now, repeat – tense those stomach muscles really tightly – hold it and feel the tension. And, let go, relax. As you breathe out, you are imagining the stress and tension being forced out of your mind and body.

'By now you should really be feeling nice and relaxed. Remember to keep your breathing nice and slow and as you breathe out, every single time, you are exhaling more and more stress and tension from your body. After every breathe out, there is less and less tension, stress and pent-up emotion left in your body.

'Now we are going to turn our attention to your arms. Start with your fingers and think about where they are and what they can feel. Now, keeping your breathing nice and slow, clench your fingers into a tight fist. Really tight so that it almost hurts. Then, just when the tension is starting to feel really uncomfortable, release all the stress in those fingers and relax them. Let them hang all floppy and loose. Enjoy the comfortable feeling of pure relaxation in your fingers. All the tension that was so uncomfortable has gone. As you breathe out, don't forget to visualize the last dregs of stress leaving your body and mind.

Now, once more, tense those fingers into a tight fist. Hold the tension. Hold it. And, relax.

'Your upper arms are next. Tense them tightly and hold them there. And, slowly, relax them. Remember, every time you breathe out you are imagining the last remnants of the emotional strains of your day being expelled from your body. Now, once more, tense those upper arm muscles and once more let the tension go. As you let the tension go, breathe out nice and slowly, visualizing the last dregs of stress being expelled from your mind.

'Now start thinking about your shoulders. How do they feel – tense or relaxed? Whatever they feel like, now you are going to really tense them by hunching up your shoulders right into your neck. Feel that tension. Feel how uncomfortable it is to feel tense in your shoulders. Hold it, and, relax them. Let them sag gently. Feel how nice it is to be relaxed. All the while as you breathe out you are imagining the very last bits of stress leaving your body. Now, once again, tense those shoulder muscles by hunching them right up to your neck. Feel that tension and hold it there for a few seconds. Now, to your relief, you can now relax them. It feels so good to relax those muscles.

'By now, you are starting to feel really good. All the tension has been breathed out and it feels so good. It's like all your problems are suddenly gone and whatever you have been worrying about has been breathed away. What a great feeling! Really enjoy that feeling of pure relaxation. Yet still, every time you breathe out you can feel the last bits of stress leave your body.

'Now we have reached your face. You are going to tense your face by screwing up your mouth, eyes and wrinkling your nose. Don't leave your forehead out – wrinkle your forehead up too. Feel that tension – it feels so uncomfortable, doesn't it? Hold it and then, let go of all that tension in your face and head – let it all go and enjoy feeling nice and relaxed. Once more, tense those muscles up – really tense them tightly until it is so uncomfortable. When you just can't hold the tension any more, let it go and relax. Relax.

'Concentrate now on your breathing again. You should be breathing nice and slowly and every time you breathe out you are breathing out stress-free pure air from your lungs. Your lungs are now stress-free – there is no more tension to breathe out. You are feeling so nice and relaxed, you should really be enjoying how your body feels and really savouring the relaxed state you are in. In a minute you will be opening your eyes, but before you do, take a minute to think about how relaxed

you are going to be for the rest of the day. If ever you start to notice that any part of your body is starting to feel tense, all you will ever need to do is say to yourself the word RE-LAX as you breathe out and you will feel nice and relaxed once more.

'Now open your eyes slowly and you can switch off the tape feeling nice and relaxed for the rest of the day.'

If you use this deep muscle relaxation technique (or other cassettes that are available from bookstores) regularly, you should experience a reduction in your blood pressure; one study that used deep muscle relaxation as part of a stress-management programme found that blood pressure was reduced after only six sessions.[5]

Visualization techniques

This is a very quick and simple approach that can provide some release of the emotional stress and can be performed anywhere – at work, on the bus home, in the lunch queue. This technique should be used after a specific situation that caused you emotional labour. You simply go through the scenario again in your mind, but this time you do not perform the emotion work. That is, in your visualization scenario, you say exactly what you feel! This allows you mentally to turn an emotionally 'dissonant' situation into an emotionally 'consonant' one (see chapter 5). Be as forceful, rude and abusive as you like! It can also help to then visualize the consequences of not performing the emotional work, ie what might have happened had you displayed the emotion that you really felt.

Case study

Mike, who purchased an electrical item from a well-known national electrical chain, told me how he used this technique to help him cope with an extremely emotionally charged situation:

'I bought a video recorder and it worked fine for eleven months. Then it started to develop an intermittent fault whereby it would simply not record programmes. I took it back under its twelve-month guarantee and they tested it. They found no fault. I explained that it was intermittent and that they needed to test it for longer, but the manager refused. He seemed to think I was trying it on. I was furious. I had a machine that I knew was faulty but no one believed me! They made me feel a fraud, but I knew I was not lying. I tried to stay calm, but when I left the store without any satisfaction, I was shaking with suppressed anger, frustration and despair. On my drive home, I re-ran the scene in my mind, but this time I released my emotions onto the manager. I called him every name under the sun and, in my mind, I had the satisfaction of seeing him cower! Of course, had I done that in real life, I would probably have been ejected from the store by security! But I felt a little calmer and was able to take practical steps to resolve the situation – eg by ringing Head Office.'

Keep an emotional labour diary

An extension of the above technique is to keep a diary of those incidents of emotional labour that cause you the most stress. Describe the scenario and write down the emotions that you felt and those that you expressed. Also write down the consequences. Then, alongside, add what might have happened had you not performed the emotion work. It is likely that, as well as acting as an emotional release, the diary will start to demonstrate how valuable your emotion work is in avoiding all the consequences that might have occurred had you not hidden your real emotions. This can help you recognize your emotion work as the skill it really is, which can be very satisfying (this will be discussed more in the next section on 'cognitive restructuring'). An example is shown below.

Scenario	Emotions I felt	Emotions I expressed	What happened	What might have happened if I hadn't managed my emotions
Had to explain yet again to subordinate how to use a simple piece of equipment.	Frustration, impatience and anger.	Patience, understanding and tolerance.	Subordinate was grateful and performed task.	Subordinate might never ask for help again and may perform tasks wrongly, or even break the equipment through misuse.
My manager came to see me just as I was trying to finish a complicated piece of work. I had to listen to his problems whilst I desperately wanted to just get on with this job so I could go home!	Frustration and impatience.	Interest and enthusiasm.	Manager finished telling me his problems and I completed my work.	My manager would have been deeply offended and that would not have helped with my desire for promotion!

Displacement

Other calming strategies, particularly when trying to dispel anger (which my research shows is the emotion that is most commonly suppressed – see chapter 7) include *displacement*, in which anger is expressed but deflected away from the person or object that provoked the negative feeling. Thus one researcher, in a study of bill collectors, noted that, after calls with abusive debtors, collectors often punched their desks and cursed the 'idiot' or 'jerk'. This often had the additional benefit of eliciting social support from other neighbouring collectors.[6] Even during a telephone conversation, displacement strategies such as making obscene gestures at the caller or even pressing the mute button before letting your real feelings out can be used (do make sure you *have* pressed the mute button!).

Hochschild's flight attendants suggested their own displacement strategies: 'I chew on ice, just crunch my anger away', 'I flush the toilet repeatedly' or 'I think about doing something mean, like pouring Ex-Lax into his coffee'.[7]

Of course, many people displace their anger at inappropriate targets, the most common of which is their partner or spouse at the end of the day. 'Stress-balls' are often marketed as a means of helping people displace their anger throughout their day to more appropriate targets. One novel displacement product on the market is a toy person whose Velcro-attached limbs can be ripped off in anger! Obviously, the aim is to displace thoughts such as 'I want to rip his head off!' from the anger-inducing person to a representation of that person whose head *can* be ripped off.

Humour

Another calming strategy is joking. The idea that joking and laughter help the release of tension was first proposed by Freud and elaborated by more modern psychologists who assert that laughter creates an 'arousal lag'[8] in which, after a brief and sharp increase in arousal (blood pressure etc) while laughing, tension then decreases dramatically. Jokes thus allow bill collectors, for instance, to release their anger rather than directing it at the abusive debtor or the next debtor. One researcher also emphasises the role of humour to diffuse emotions, this time of embarrassment, amongst wheelchair users: 'A wheelchair user's potentially embarrassing situation often provokes anxiety in witnesses to her or his plight. Defining the situation as laughable can ease everyone's particular "dis-ease" '.[9] For instance, one wheelchair user whose leg had been amputated was asked by a child (much to its parents' chagrin) where his leg was. The amputee answered, 'It's gone. If you find it, I'll give you fifty cents. I've been looking for that damned thing all week!'[9]

Humour is also frequently used in the medical profession by doctors and nurses who are continually faced with the most emotionally demanding situations. For instance, they might give patients (or, in the case of medical students, cadavers) an amusing nickname, tell 'black' or 'sick' jokes about patients' conditions, or laugh about minor mistakes they might have made.

COGNITIVE RESTRUCTURING

Cognitive restructuring refers to the mental act that we can perform to change the way we view or see something. It can help us see the good in the bad, or make us realize that things are not as bad as they may seem. For instance, imagine that you learn that you are to be made redundant. This is, obviously, a tremendously negative event, but by cognitively restructuring the event, it could be seen instead as an opportunity to set up independently, to go freelance, develop a new business idea – even to have a baby! The event has stayed the same – the redundancy is still there – but the way it is viewed has changed. This is cognitive restructuring.

With emotional labour performance, cognitive restructuring can be used in a number of helpful ways:

Restructuring view of emotion work

Many people view emotion work in a negative light, as being unskilled labour that they resent doing. Acting or being phony are seen negatively, as something to be ashamed of and embarrassed about. Most people (other than professional actors) prefer to think that they are 'themselves' at work and that they are able to act in a natural way, rather than putting on an act or taking on roles.

However, the reality is that many of us do put on acts or take on roles as part of the impression-management techniques that we are all naturally involved in. To some degree, we are all social actors, trying to create certain impressions of ourselves or our organization. If we could start to acknowledge our emotional labour as skilled acting work, instead of unskilled faking, then we would feel more positive about this aspect of our work and would cope better with the stress. As one source puts it, 'the best copers . . . are those who see the job as all about acting; they treat the emotional performance as a game into which they can switch in or out'.[10]

Research carried out on police detectives in America reveals very clearly how this reframing of emotion work changes the labour from being viewed as unskilled to skilled work. The detectives, as discussed in chapter 3, must often play 'good cop/bad cop'-type roles in order to elicit confessions from criminals. Instead of seeing this as unskilled emotion work, they view it as 'higher status mental work' enabling them to see their encounters with criminals as 'challenging intellectual games'.[11]

The effectiveness of this technique is shown in the following case study:

Case study

Steve works in a customer service role and often has to deal with irate customers. He says:

'I often imagine that I am an actor and that the skill of my work comes from being able to give a credible performance. If a customer is complaining, I imagine that the sympathy I display is being judged and that an imaginary audience will regard me highly for the skilled acting I have demonstrated.'

Restructuring view of the incident

The second way in which cognitive restructuring can be used is in restructuring the way the emotion-evoking incident is viewed so that different emotions can be evoked. For instance, flight attendants are encouraged to see a 'passenger demanding constant attention' not as an irritant who arouses anger, but as someone with problems that may be causing them to behave as they do. Thus, for instance, the passenger may be afraid of flying, or have just had a row with their spouse. In this way, the flight attendants are urged to 'pretend something traumatic has happened in their lives' so that they will be able to replace their anger with sympathy.[7] By focusing on the customer or passenger, the worker is able to restructure their natural emotional response.

Self-talk

Self-talk is described as 'intermittent mental monologue' that most people conduct about the events they experience and their reaction to those events. For instance, in Hochschild's book *The Managed Heart*, she found that flight attendants frequently coped with the emotional strain by reminding themselves that the shift would soon be over. 'you can say to yourself, it's half an hour to go, now it's twenty-nine minutes.'[7] Another example was given to me by a sales assistant for a national clothes chain whom I interviewed:

'This customer bought fifty pounds' worth of children's clothes and asked if she could keep the hangers. I explained, very politely, that at the moment we were really short of children's hangers and that we couldn't even put out new stock because we didn't have enough hangers. She started shouting at me, saying she couldn't believe it and that by buying the clothes, she was effectively buying the hangers. I explained, still smiling, that the hangers were free and not part of the price, but that we just couldn't spare them. She was furious and insisted on taking my name and the address of head office. She told me I would be out of a job and even called me a cow. I kept smiling and did not rise to the bait. But when she left, I had to leave my post – I ran up to the staff room, stomping on each stair as I went, slammed a few doors and kept telling myself that she was only one customer, that I would be going home soon, that I had done nothing wrong. I then felt able to return to my post.'

The point about self-talk is that it should be reassuring and rational whilst helping you to view the incident differently.

CONCLUSION

Hiding what we feel and faking what we don't is shown in this book to be an increasingly common feature of organizational life. Some may resist it, decry it or otherwise accuse emotion managers of being fake, false and phony. To some extent, this may be true, as acting becomes as recognized a skill at work as communicating, word processing or team leading. However, as long as the acting is performed in 'good faith', ie without deceitful or malicious intent, I believe this new trend to be good, not bad. Anything that acknowledges the role of emotions at work and the increasing need to control our emotional front can only be of benefit to the employer, the employed and to customers and colleagues. Anything that recognizes that the demand to genuinely feel desired emotions at all times is an impossible demand has to be a good thing. However, this move towards a scripted society is not without its costs, and the benefits of celebrating emotion management must be tempered with a healthy respect for the potential disadvantages too. It is not the aim of this book to encourage workers to fake and hide if this causes them even more stress, leads them to feel even more burned out and causes them to be even more susceptible to illness than they already are. Emotion management should go hand-in-hand with the various coping strategies outlined in this book. What is needed is a partnership, a balance between the emotional demands on the one hand, and the need to retain a sense of the self, a chance to feel and display true feelings on the other. This should, ultimately, involve cooperation between employer and employed so that rather than the worker's ability to hide and fake being exploited, as many believe it is to some extent now, it is instead channelled and managed to the benefit of all.

NOTES

CHAPTER 1: EMOTION AT WORK – A NECESSARY EVIL OR A VALUABLE ASSET?

[1] Putnam, L L and Mumby, D K, 'Organizations, emotion and the myth of rationality', in S Fineman (ed), *Emotion in Organizations*, Sage, London, 1993

[2] James, N, 'Emotional labour: skill and work in the social regulation of feelings', *Sociological Review*, 37, pp15–42, 1989

[3] Meyerson, D E, 'Uncovering socially undesirable emotions: experiences of ambiguity in organizations', *American Behavioral Scientist*, 33, pp296–307, 1990

[4] Oatley, K, 'State of the art: emotion', *The Psychologist*, 11 (6), p285, 1998

[5] James, W, 'What is an emotion?', *Mind*, 9, pp188–205, 1884

[6] Laird, J D, 'Self-attribution of emotion: the effects of facial expression on the quality of emotional experience', *Journal of Personality and Social Psychology*, 29, pp475–86, 1974

[7] Cannon, W B, 'The James-Lange theory of emotions: a critical examination and an alternative', *American Journal of Psychology*, 39, pp106–24, 1927

[8] Shachter, S and Singer, J E, 'Cognitive, social and psychological determinants of emotional state', *Psychological Review*, 69, pp379–99, 1962

[9] Dutton, D C and Aron, A P, 'Some evidence for heightened sexual attraction under conditions of high anxiety', *Journal of Personality and Social Psychology*, 30, pp510–17, 1974

[10] Matsumoto, D, 'Cultural similarities and differences in display rules', *Motivation & Emotion*, 14, pp195–214, 1990

[11] Pollack, L H and Thoits, P A, 'Process in emotional socialization', *Social Psychology Quarterly*, 52 (1), pp22–34, 1989

[12] Darwin, C, *The Expression of the Emotions in Man and Animals* (new edition with commentaries by P Ekman), Oxford University Press, New York, 1988

[13] Smith, T, 'Severe life stress, major depression and emotion-related negative memory', in N H Frijda (ed), *Proceedings of the 9th Conference of the International Society for Research on Emotions*, pp416–20, ISRE Publications, Toronto, 1996

[14] Maslow, A, *Motivation and Personality*, Harper and Row, New York, 1954

[15] Bennis, W and Townsend, R, *Reinventing Leadership*, p29, Judy Piatkus, London, 1985

[16] Hooper, A and Potter, J, *The Business of Leadership: Adding Lasting Value to Your Organization*, Ashgate Publishing, Aldershot, 1997

[17] Hatfield, E, Cacioppo, J and Rapson, R L, 'Primitive emotional contagion', in M S Clark (ed), *Review of Personality and Social Psychology*, 14, pp151–77, Sage, Newbury Park, California

[18] Goleman, D, *Emotional Intelligence: why it can matter more than IQ*, p115, Bloomsbury, London, 1996

[19] Ashforth, B and Humphrey, R, 'Emotion in the workplace: a reappraisal', *Human Relations*, 48 (2), pp97–125, 1995

[20] Arther, R O and Caputo, R R, *Interrogation for Investigators*, William C Copp & Associates, New York, 1959

[21] Hayano, D M, *Poker Faces*, University of California Press, Berkeley, 1982

[22] Bradshaw, D, 'Sister, can you spare a smile?', *New York*, 13 (8), p7, 1980

CHAPTER 2: THE 'HAVE A NICE DAY' CULTURE: EMOTIONAL CONTROL AT WORK

[1] Wharton, A S and Erickson, R J, 'Managing emotion on the job and at home: understanding the consequences of multiple emotional roles', *Academy of Management Review*, 18 (3), pp457–86, 1993

[2] and [3] Hochschild, A, *The Managed Heart: commercialization of human feeling*, University of California Press, Berkeley, 1983

[4] Newton, T, *Managing Stress: emotion and power at work*, Sage, London, 1995

[5] Wilson, G, *Psychology for Performing Artists: butterflies and bouquets*, Jessica Kingsley, London, 1994

[6] Temoshok, L and Dreher, H, *The Type C Connection: the behavioral links to cancer and your health*, Random House, New York, 1992

[7] Ashforth, B and Humphrey, R, 'Emotional labor in service roles: the influence of identity', *Academy of Management Review*, 18 (1), pp86–115, 1993

[8] and [9] Rafaeli, A and Sutton, R I, 'The expression of emotion in organizational life', in L L Cummings and B M Staw (eds), *Research in Organizational Behavior*, 11, pp1–42, 1989

[10] Taylor, G, 'Put on a happy face – culture, identity and performance in the service role', paper presented at 'Tourism and Culture: Towards the 21st Century' conference at University of Northumbria at Newcastle, September 1996

[11] Frijda, N H, *The Emotions*, Cambridge University Press, Cambridge, Massachusetts, 1986

[12] Dare Hall, Zoe, 'Please don't tell me to have a nice day', in *Daily Express*, 26 January 1998

[13] Brand, J, *Event Magazine*, issue 6, p13, 8–21 May 1997

[14] Thompson, V A, *Bureaucracy and the Modern World*, General Learning Press, Morristown, New York, 1976

[15] Judi James of the Industrial Society quoted in the *Daily Mail*'s Career Mail, 22 February 1996

[16] Mann, S, 'Customer expectations of the emotional display of service providers', paper presented at the 12th Annual Conference of the Society of Industrial and Occupational Psychology Conference, St Louis, Missouri, USA, 1997

[17] Mann, S and Shinner, T, 'Expectations of emotional displays in the workplace; an Australian/British comparative study', paper presented at the Australian Industrial and Occupational Psychology Annual Conference, Melbourne, Australia, 1997

[18] Mann, S, 'Don't tell me to "have a nice day"', paper presented at the annual conference of the British Psychological Society Division of Occupational Psychology, Eastbourne, UK, 1998

[19] Mann, S, Jones, R, Rafaeli, A and Shinner, T, 'Faking it at work; emotional display v real feeling. An American, Australian, British and Israeli comparative study', paper presented at the International Association of Applied Psychology Conference, San Francisco, USA, 1998

[20] Mann, S, 'Communicating emotions across the customer–organization boundary; what do customers really expect? An Israeli-American comparative study', paper presented at the 48th Annual Conference of the International Communication Association, Jerusalem, Israel, 1998

[21] Tolich, M B, 'Alienating and liberating emotions at work: supermarket clerks' performance of customer service', *Journal of Contemporary Ethnography*, 22 (3), pp361–81, 1993

[22] Parkinson, B, 'Emotional stylists: strategies of expressive management among trainee hairdressers', *Cognition and Emotion*, 5 (5/6), pp419–34, 1991

[23] Albrecht, K and Zemke, R, *Service America! Doing business in the new economy*, Dow Jones-Irwin, Homewood, Illinois, 1985

[24] Noon, M and Blyton, P, *The Realities of Work*, Macmillan, London, 1997

[25] Goleman, D, *Emotional Intelligence: why it matters more than IQ*, Bloomsbury, London, 1996

[26] Hall cited in Rafaeli, A and Sutton, R I, 'Expression of emotion as a part of the work role', *Academy of Management Review*, 12, pp23–37, 1987

CHAPTER 3: 'HAVE A ROTTEN DAY!' – AND OTHER SCRIPTED CULTURES

[1] Rachel Pugh, 'Have a nice day, honest!' *Manchester Evening News*, 1998

[2] Ritzer, G, *The McDonaldization of Society*, Pine Forge Press, California, 1992

[3] Hochschild, A, *The Managed Heart: commercialization of human feeling*, University of California Press, Berkeley, 1983

[4] Leidner, R, 'Selling hamburgers and selling insurance: gender, work and identity in interactive service jobs', *Gender & Society*, 5, pp154–77, 1991

[5] Van Maanen, J and Kunda, G, 'Real feelings: emotional expression and organizational culture', in L L Cummings and B M Staw (eds), *Research in Organizational Behavior*, 11, pp43–103, JAI Press, Greenwich, Connecticut, 1989

[6] Rafaeli, A and Sutton, R I, 'Expression of emotion as a part of the work role', *Academy of Management Review*, 12, pp23–37, 1987

[7] Advert by Kinsman Reynolds Consulting in *Australia New Zealand Travel Planner*, No 15, April–May 1997

[8] Hall, E, 'Smiling, deferring and flirting: doing gender by giving good service', *Work and Occupations*, 20 (4), pp452–71, 1993

[9] Ekman, P, *Telling Lies*, Berkeley Books, New York, 1985

[10] Cahill, S E and Eggleston, R, 'Managing emotions in public: the case of wheelchair users', *Social Psychology Quarterly*, 57 (4), pp300–12, 1994

[11] Temoshok, L and Dreher, H, *The Type C Connection: the behavioral links to cancer and your health*, Random House, New York, 1992

[12] Jackall, R, *Moral Mazes: the world of corporate managers*, Oxford University Press, New York, 1988

[13] Smith, A C and Kleinman, S, 'Managing emotions in medical school: students' contacts with the living and the dead', *Social Psychology Quarterly*, 52, pp56–69, 1989

[14] Rafaeli, A and Sutton, R I, 'The expression of emotion in organizational life', in L L Cummings and B M Staw (eds), *Research in Organizational Behavior*, 11, pp1–42, 1989

[15] Sutton, R J, 'Maintaining norms about expressed emotions: the case of bill collectors', *Administrative Science Quarterly*, 36, pp245–68, 1991

[16] Stenross, B and Kleinman, S, 'The highs and lows of emotional labor: detectives' encounters with criminals and victims', *Journal of Contemporary Ethnography*, 17, pp435–52, 1989

[17] Hickey, J V, Thompson, W E and Foster, D L, 'Becoming the Easter Bunny: socialization into a fantasy role', *Journal of Contemporary Ethnography*, 17, pp67–95, 1988

[18] Pogrebin M R and Poole E D, 'Humor in the briefing room: a study of the strategic use of humor among the police', *Journal of Contemporary Ethnography*, 17, pp183–210, 1988

[19] Jones, Y, 'Occupational stress amongst GPs', *The Occupational Psychologist*, 1996

[20] Tolich, M B, 'Alienating and liberating emotions at work: supermarket clerks' performance of customer service', *Journal of Contemporary Ethnography*, 22 (3), pp361–81, 1993

[21] Wilson, G, *The Psychology of the Performing Arts*, Croom Helm, Kent, 1985

[22] Donnelly, G, 'My best acting is as a dad!' *Woman's Own*, pp24–5, 8 June 1998

CHAPTER 4: BECOMING A ONE-MINUTE FRIEND – HOW TO MANAGE YOUR EMOTIONS TO GET THE JOB AND KEEP THE JOB.

[1] Forbes, R J and Jackson, P R, 'Non-verbal behavior and the outcomes of selection interviews', *Journal of Occupational Psychology*, 53, pp65–72, 1980

[2] Boas, M and Chain, S, *Big Mac: the unauthorized story of McDonald's*, Dutton, New York, 1976

[3] Hochschild, A, *The Managed Heart: commercialization of human feeling*, University of California Press, Berkeley, 1983

[4] Taylor, G, ' "Put on a happy face" – culture, identity and performance in the service role', paper presented at 'Tourism and Culture: Towards the 21st Century' conference at University of Northumbria at Newcastle, September 1996

[5] Sutton, R J, 'Maintaining norms about expressed emotions: the case of bill collectors', *Administrative Science Quarterly*, 36, pp245–68, 1991

[6] Rafaeli, A and Sutton, R I, 'The expression of emotion in organizational life', in L L Cummings and B M Staw (eds), *Research in Organizational Behavior*, 11, pp1–42, 1989

[7] Peters, T J and Waterman, R H Jnr, *In Search of Excellence*, Harper & Row, New York, 1982

[8] Tyler, S (producer) and Nathan, J (producer), *In Search of Excellence* (film), Public Broadcast System, New York, 1985

[9] Walt Disney Productions, *Your Role in the Walt Disney World Show*, Walt Disney Productions, Orlando, Florida, 1982

[10] Tolich, M B, 'Alienating and liberating emotions at work: supermarket clerks' performance of customer service', *Journal of Contemporary Ethnography*, 22 (3), pp361–81, 1993

[11] Daniels, M J, 'Affect and its control in the medical intern', *American Journal of Sociology*, 66, pp259–67, 1960

[12] Sutton, R I and Rafaeli, A, 'Untangling the relationship between displayed emotions and organizational sales: the case of convenience stores', *Academy of Management Journal*, 31 (3), pp461–87, 1988

CHAPTER 5: 'EMOTIONAL LABOUR' – THE MENTAL EFFORT INVOLVED IN MANAGING YOUR EMOTIONS

[1] Newton, T, *Managing Stress: emotion and power at work*, Sage, London, 1995

[2] Hochschild, A, *The Managed Heart: commercialization of human feeling*, University of California Press, Berkeley, 1983

[3] Mars, G and Nicod, M, *The World of Waiters*, George Allen & Unwin, London, 1984

[4] Rafaeli, A and Sutton, R I, 'The expression of emotion in organizational life', in L L Cummings and B M Staw (eds), *Research in Organizational Behavior*, 11, pp1–42, 1989

[5] Parkinson, B, 'Emotional stylists: strategies of expressive management among trainee hairdressers', *Cognition and Emotion*, 5 (5/6), pp419–34, 1991

[6] Putnam, L L and Mumby, D K, 'Organizations, emotion and the myth of rationality', in S. Fineman (ed), *Emotion in Organizations*, Sage, London, 1993

[7] Briner, R B, 'Beyond stress and satisfaction: understanding and managing emotions at work', paper submitted to EAWOP Conference, Gyor, Hungary, 1995

[8] Spradley, J P and Mann, B, *The Cocktail Waitress*, Wiley, New York, 1975

[9] Jones, Y, 'Occupational stress amongst GPs', *The Occupational Psychologist*, 1996

[10] Dunkerley, D, *The Foreman*, Routledge & Kegan Paul, London, 1975

[11] Martin, S E, *Breaking and entering: policewomen on patrol*, University of California Press, Berkeley, 1980

[12] Sutton, R J, 'Maintaining norms about expressed emotions: the case of bill collectors', *Administrative Science Quarterly*, 36, pp245–68, 1991

[13] James, N, 'Divisions of emotional labour', in S. Fineman (ed), *Emotion in Organizations*, Sage, London, 1993

[14] Linstead cited in Noon, M and Blyton, P, *The Realities of Work*, Macmillan, London, 1997

[15] Sutton, R I and Rafaeli, A, 'Untangling the relationship between displayed emotions and organizational sales: the case of convenience stores', *Academy of Management Journal*, 31 (3), pp461–87, 1988

[16] Tolich, M B, 'Alienating and liberating emotions at work: supermarket clerks' performance of customer service', *Journal of Contemporary Ethnography*, 22 (3), pp361–81, 1993

[17] Noon, M and Blyton, P, *The Realities of Work*, Macmillan, London, 1997

[18] Rafaeli, A and Sutton, R I, 'Expression of emotion as a part of the work role', *Academy of Management Review*, 12, pp23–37, 1987

[19] Isen, A M and Shalker, T E, 'The effect of feeling state on evaluation of positive, neutral and negative stimuli: when you "accentuate the positive" do you "eliminate the negative"?' *Social Psychology Quarterly*, 45, pp58–63, 1982

[20] Westbrook, R A, 'Intrapersonal affective influences on consumer satisfaction with products', *Journal of Consumer Research*, 7, pp49–54, 1980

[21] Dowling, G R, *Corporate Reputations*, Kogan Page, London, 1984

[22] Bromley, D B, *Reputation, Image and Impression Management*, Wiley, London, 1993

[23] Scott, M J and Stradling, S G, *Counselling for Post-Traumatic Stress Disorder*, Sage, London, 1992

[24] Guthrie, T, quoted in Snyder, M, *Public Appearances/Private Realities: the psychology of self-monitoring*, W H Freeman, New York, 1986

[25] Wilson, G, *The Psychology of the Performing Arts*, Croom Helm, Kent, 1985

[26] Zajonc, R B, 'Emotion and facial efference: an ignored theory reclaimed', *Science*, 15–21 April 1985

[27] Hatfield, E, Cacioppo, J and Rapson, R L, 'Primitive emotional contagion', in M S Clark (ed), *Review of Personality and Social Psychology*, 14, pp151–177, Sage, Newbury Park, California, 1992

[28] Frijda, N H, (1986), *The Emotions*, Cambridge University Press, Cambridge, Massachusetts, 1986

CHAPTER 6: THE 'HAVE A NICE DAY' SYNDROME

[1] Newton, T, *Managing Stress: emotion and power at work*, Sage, London, 1995

[2] Cited in Temoshok, L and Dreher, H, *The Type C Connection: the behavioral links to cancer and your health*, Random House, New York, 1992

[3] Wharton, A S, 'The affective consequences of service work: managing emotions on the job', *Work and Occupations*, 20, pp205–32, 1993

[4] Hochschild, A, *The Managed Heart: commercialization of human feeling*, University of California Press, Berkeley, 1983

[5] Parkinson, B, 'Emotional stylists: strategies of expressive management among trainee hairdressers', *Cognition and Emotion*, 5 (5/6), pp419–34, 1991

[6] Festinger, B, *A Theory of Cognitive Dissonance*, Row, Peterson, Evanston, Illinois, 1957

[7] Milbank, D, ' "New-collar" work', *The Wall Street Journal*, ppA1, 9 September 1993

[8] Sutton, R J, 'Maintaining norms about expressed emotions: the case of bill collectors', *Administrative Science Quarterly*, 36, pp245–68, 1991

[9] Hochschild, A, 'Emotion work, feeling rules and social structure', *American Journal of Sociology*, 85, pp551–75, 1979

[10] James, N, 'Emotional labour: skill and work in the social regulation of feelings', *Sociological Review*, 37, pp15–42, 1989

[11] Stenross, B and Kleinman, S, 'The highs and lows of emotional labor: detectives' encounters with criminals and victims', *Journal of Contemporary Ethnography*, 17, pp435–52, 1989

[12] Van Maanen, J and Kunda, G, 'Real feelings: emotional expression and organizational culture', in L L Cummings and B M Staw (eds), *Research in Organizational Behavior*, 11, 1989

[13] Ashforth, B and Humphrey, R, 'Emotional labor in service roles: the 1influence of identity', *Academy of Management Review*, 18 (1), pp86–115, 1993

[14] Foegen, J H, 'Hypocrisy pay', *Employee Responsibilities and Rights Journal*, 1, pp85–7, 1988

[15] Maslach, C and Jackson, S E, 'The measurement of experienced burnout', *Journal of Occupational Behavior*, 2, pp99–113, 1981

[16] Maslach, C, 'Understanding burnout: definitional issues in analyzing a complex phenomenon', in Wharton Stewart Paine (ed), *Job Stress & Burnout*, Sage, California, 1983

[17] Jourard, S M, 'Healthy personality and self-disclosure', *Mental Hygiene*, 43, 1959

[18] Freud, S, *Jokes and their Relations to the Unconscious*, Pergamon Press, London, 1960

[19] Alexander, R, 'Psychological aspects of medicine', *Psychological Medicine*, 1, 7–18, 1939

[20] Beutler, L E, Engle D, Oro-Beutler M E, Daldrup R and Meredith K, 'Inability to express intense affect: a common link between depression and pain', *Journal of Consulting and Clinical Psychology*, 54, pp752–9, 1986

[21] Pelletier, K R, *Mind as Healer, Mind as Slayer*, Delacorte Press, New York, 1985

[22] Udelman, H D and Udelman, D L, 'Emotions and rheumatological disorders', *American Journal of Psychotherapy*, 1981

[23] Pennebaker, J W, *The Psychology of Physical Symptoms*, Springer-Verlag, New York, 1982

[24] Goleman, D, *Emotional Intelligence: why it can matter more than IQ*, Bloomsbury, London, 1996

[25] Cox, T and McCay, C, 'Psychosocial factors and psychophysiological mechanisms in the etiology and development of cancers', *Social Science and Medicine*, 16, pp381–96, 1982

[26] In [2]

[27] Appel, M A, Holroyd, K A and Gorkin, L, 'Anger and the etiology and progression of physical disease', in L Temoshok, C van Dyke and L Zegans (eds), *Emotions in Health & Illness: theoretical and research foundations*, pp73–87, Grove & Stratton, New York, 1983

[28] Friedman, H S and Booth-Kewley, S, 'Personality, Type A behavior and coronary heart disease: the role of emotional expression', *Journal of Personality and Social Psychology*, 53, pp783–92, 1987

[29] Friedman, H S, Hall, J A and Harris, M J, 'Type A behavior, nonverbal expressive style and health', *Journal of Personality and Social Psychology*, 48, pp1299–315, 1985

[30] Gentry, W D, 'Relationship of anger-coping styles and blood pressure among Black Americans', in MA Chesney and R H Rosenman (eds), *Anger and Hostility in Cardiovascular and Behavioral Disorders*, pp139–48, Hemisphere, New York, 1985

[31] King L A and Emmons R A, 'Conflict over emotional expression: psychological and physical correlates', *Journal of Personality and Social Psychology*, 58 (5), pp864–77, 1990

[32] Rutter D R and Fielding P J, 'Sources of occupational stress: an examination of British police officers', *Work and Stress*, 2, pp291–99, 1988

[33] Mann, S, 'Achieving corporate communication excellence: the cost to health', Tenth Conference on Corporate Communications, Fairleigh Dickenson University, New Jersey, USA, 1997

[34] Quick, J C and Quick J D, *Organizational Stress and Preventative Management*, McGraw-Hill, New York, 1984

[35] Snyder, M, *Public Appearances/Private Realities: the psychology of self-monitoring*, WH Freeman, New York, 1986

[36] Mann, S, 'Are we smiling on the outside but screaming on the inside?', *Club Sirius* magazine, issue 4, 1998

CHAPTER 7: OUR SECRET EMOTIONAL LIVES AT WORK

[1] Mann, S, 'All the world's a stage: the emotional labour of workplace communications', unpublished PhD thesis, University of Salford, UK, 1997

[2] Hochschild, A, *The Managed Heart: commercialization of human feeling*. University of California Press, Berkeley, 1983

[3] Van Maanen, J and Kunda, G, 'Real feelings: emotional expression and organizational culture', in L L Cummings and B M Staw (eds), *Research in Organizational Behavior*, 11, 1989

[4] Lawrence, M, 'When the stiff upper lip slips' (article on the author's research), the *Guardian*, 22 June 1998

[5] Fisher, C D, 'Boredom at work: a neglected concept' *Human Relations*, 46, pp395–417, 1993

[6] Grzyb, J, 'Keep on smiling', *Cosmopolitan*, August, 1997

[7] Rafaeli, A and Sutton, R I, 'The expression of emotion in organizational life', in L L Cummings and B M Staw (eds), *Research in Organizational Behavior*, 11, pp1–42, 1989

[8] Foster, T R V, *101 Great Mission Statements· how the world's leading companies run their business*, Kogan Page, London, 1993

[9] Boas, M and Chain, S, *Big Mac: the unauthorized story of McDonald's*, Dutton, New York, 1976

Chapter 8: Coping Strategies For The 'Have A Nice Day' Syndrome

[1] James, N, 'Emotional labour: skill and work in the social regulation of feelings', *Sociological Review*, 37, pp15–42 1989

[2] Mann, S, 'Faking can be dangerous to your health', *Reference Book for Employers Magazine*, 1 (1), pp14–18 1997

[3] Mann, S, 'The "Have a Nice Day" syndrome: how being nice can affect your employee's health', *Professional Manager*, 7 (2), pp20–1, 1998

[4] Bailey, J, 'Service agents, emotional labor and costs to overall customer service', paper presented at the 11th Annual Conference of the American Society for Industrial and Occupational Psychology, San Diego, April 1996

[5] Tisdelle, D A, Hansen D J, St Lawrence, J S and Brown, J C, 'Stress management training for dental students', *Journal of Dental Education*, 48, pp196–201, 1984

[6] Sutton, R J, 'Maintaining norms about expressed emotions: the case of bill collectors', *Administrative Science Quarterly*, 36, pp245–268, 1991

[7] Hochschild, A, *The Managed Heart: commercialization of human feeling*, University of California Press, Berkeley, 1983

[8] Berlyne, D E, 1969 'Laughter, humor and play', in Gardner L and Aronson, E (eds), *Handbook of Social Psychology*, pp795–852, Addison-Wesley, Reading, Massachusetts, 1969

[9] Cahill, S E and Eggleston, R 'Managing emotions in public: the case of wheelchair users', *Social Psychology Quarterly*, 57 (4), pp300–312, 1994

[10] Noon, M and Blyton, P, *The Realities of Work*, Macmillan, London, 1997

[11] Stenross, B and Kleinman, S, 'The highs and lows of emotional labor: detectives' encounters with criminals and victims', *Journal of Contemporary Ethnography*, 17, pp435–52, 1989

Further Reading

The following texts may be useful to help you cope with stress over and above those strategies recommended in this book. They should also encourage you to understand the negative consequences of stress and so encourage you to tackle it positively.

Carrington, P, *The Power of Letting Go*, Element, Shaftesbury, 1999

Cartright, S and Cooper, C L, *No Hassle!: taking the stress out of work*, Century Business, London, 1994

Chandra, P, *The Complete Guide to Stress Management*, Optima, London, 1996

Lovelace, R T, *Stressmaster*, Wiley, New York, 1988

Markham, U, *Managing Stress*, Element, Shaftesbury, 1993

Rowsham, Arthur, *Stress: an owner's manual*, Oneworld, Oxford, 1993 (reissued 1997)

Sapolsky, R M, *Why Zebras Don't Get Ulcers: a guide to stress and stress-related diseases*, Freeman, New York, 1994

Audiocassettes

Carrington, P, *Learn to Meditate Kit*, Element, Shaftesbury, 1998

Useful Addresses

I am keen to collect personal anecdotes or stories about readers' experiences with hiding or faking emotions at work. Please send your stories to:

Dr Sandi Mann
Department of Psychology
University of Central Lancashire
Preston PR1 2HE
United Kingdom

or e-mail them to:

s.mann@uclan.ac.uk

If you would like further copies of the MERI™ questionnaire or would like a feedback report and analysis of your own emotional labour or emotion management, please contact Ward Dutton International at:

Ward Dutton International
Hill Farmhouse
Chishill Road
Heydon
Nr Royston
Hertfordshire SG8 8PW
UK
(Tel 01763 837111)

INDEX